The Songwriters

TONY STAVEACRE

The
Songwriters

BRITISH BROADCASTING CORPORATION

The Songwriters originated in a series of eight television programmes of the same title which were first broadcast on BBC 1 in the spring of 1978. The director was Keith Cheetham, assisted by Stephany Marks; and the programme research was compiled by Helen Morton, who also helped to prepare this book. The songs were brought to life by a company of singer/actors including Colin Bennett, Peter Gale, Sheila White, Marti Webb, Paul Jones, Angela Richards and Marilyn Hill-Smith. Musical direction was by Ken Moule and Peter Martin.

Published by the
British Broadcasting Corporation
35 Marylebone High Street
London W1M 4AA

ISBN 0 563 17638 5
© Tony Staveacre 1980

Printed in England
by Jolly & Barber Ltd, Rugby

Contents

INTRODUCTION
7

LESLIE STUART
'The Lily of Laguna'
11

LIONEL MONCKTON
'Arcady is Ever Young'
33

NOËL COWARD
'Poor Little Rich Girl'
57

RAY NOBLE
'Goodnight Sweetheart'
73

IVOR NOVELLO
'We'll Gather Lilacs'
95

LIONEL BART
'Fings Ain't Wot They Used T'Be'
121

JOHN LENNON
AND PAUL MCCARTNEY
'A Hard Day's Night'
141

TIM RICE AND
ANDREW LLOYD WEBBER
'Heaven on Their Minds'
167

ACKNOWLEDGEMENTS
Picture Credits and Song Credits
190

Introduction

In the music-hall, a song usually had two parts – a verse, then a chorus, in alternating pattern. Each verse was different, while the chorus remained the same. The verse told the *story* of the song and got the audience settled. Sometimes it was half-spoken 'recitative' – against a musical background that discreetly signalled the melody that was coming. At the end of the verse – a pause, and then the orchestra would usher in the inescapable chorus, of which the most important element was a *good tune*. It was catchy, infectious, and soon the audience would be humming along. When the singer went back to the verse to pick up the story, the audience would now be poised, waiting for the moment when the song would slide effortlessly into that *tune* again, and they could relax and go along with it. The third time round, with the tempo increasing, they would be raring to go: it only needed the singer to make the inevitable invitation – 'All together now!' – and they were off, singing the song as if they'd known it all their lives, with the singer shouting each line a few bars early, to jog their memory. A couple of encores, and by the time they left the theatre, they knew it by heart.

Which was just what the songwriter (and the publisher, and the songcover artist, and the singer who'd bought it) wanted. If people sang it at home, at work, in the street, others would pick it up, others would buy the music, and soon the whole world would be singing 'Ta-ra-ra Boom-de-ay!' which 'lit at the red skirts of Lottie Collins, spread like a dancing flame through the land, obsessing the minds of young and old until it became a veritable song-pest. . . .'

Lottie Collins is dead, music-hall is finished, but still the song survives, passed on by 'word of mouth' from generation to generation, sung by grannies to their grandchildren, taught by musicians to their pupils.

Music-hall audience photographed at the last night of the Canterbury, May 1912

Along the way, the verse gets forgotten. So the story is lost. What remains is a memorable, singable *tune* and some words that fit it neatly. Styles of singing change, as performers adapt their material to the new media, and 'live' theatre gives way to electronic reproduction. Now a song that once depended on a particular context, style or accent, loses its meaning altogether. The lament of a negro boy pining for his sweetheart – 'it's de same old tale of a palpatating nigger, dat wants to be married very soon' – becomes a gentle, pointless love lyric, sung in the smoothest of tones – 'I know she loves me, because she said so'. Of all the girls who have been lovingly compared to the Lily of Laguna, how many knew that she started life as a negro shepherdess, living wild in a cave in Mississippi?

In their original form, the songs reflect their times. Like musical journalists, the songwriters reveal the moods and preoccupation of their day. They feed the public appetite for new tastes and sensations. They indulge our need for reassurance, escapism, nostalgia, romance. They make us laugh, they make us cry. And if they strike the right note, they make themselves a fortune. But the exact combination of ingredients that makes a song a 'hit' remains infuriatingly unpredictable. The birth of a song, the moment at which it first catches the public imagination, is often due to a unique coincidence of changing fashion, technical innovation, and pure fancy: which produces, in 'The Lily of Laguna', a perfect child of the Victorian era – just as 'Poor Little Rich Girl' *belongs* to the 1920s, and 'Eleanor Rigby' to the 1960s.

These 'incidentals' are the beads on which the theme of this book is threaded. They provide the link between eight generations of songwriters, each of whom enjoyed a period of furious creative activity (seven years seems to be the norm), and dominated the popular music scene for a decade. Apart from that, they would appear to have little in common, except of course that elusive, special skill – the ability to produce a combination of words and music that will stick in the listener's mind like a burr, never to be forgotten. I am confident that the reader will be able to supply his own mental sound-track to these ostensibly silent pages.

Tony Staveacre
Blagdon, Avon
March 1979

LESLIE STUART

'The Lily of Laguna'

On a poster for the Oxford Music-Hall in 1899, it was billed as 'a new song scene of the American cotton fields written by Mr Leslie Stuart and sung by Mr Eugene Stratton'. W. Macqueen-Pope provides a vivid description of that first performance:

'There he was, a coon carried away in an ecstasy of love, discovered as the curtain rose sitting on a gate, whittling away at a stick while the orchestra very softly played the introduction and the verse. But his thoughts were far away: he whittled that stick by sheer force of habit, without knowing what he was doing, his mind fixed on his Lily Girl – his shepherdess . . . And then when the tension of watching that silent dreaming figure could hardly be borne, he would begin, very softly, to speak his thoughts, intertwined with Stuart's wonderful melody.'

It was the strangest of combinations: an imitation negro song from the Deep South, sung by a white American from Buffalo, of German parentage, and written by a church organist from Lancashire, whose father was Irish. But Leslie Stuart felt a real affinity towards the people of the American Southern States, whose history and mythology were to provide him with a potent source of inspiration.

The fascination took hold of him in childhood. His father bore a striking resemblance to Buffalo Bill – as a result of which he was a well-known figure in Liverpool, where he worked as property-master at the old Amphitheatre. Leslie Stuart was born in Southport in 1856, or 1862, or 1864: by his own account, the church where he was baptised was burnt down, so there's no official record of his birth. His real name was Thomas Barrett. At the age of three he had his first glimpse of the magical world of Victorian theatre, from an orange box high in the flies.

11

The original song-cover of 'The Lily of Laguna',
showing Eugene Stratton in character

He was also introduced to another world of make-believe and fantasy, in the American adventure stories which his father loved to read him: tales of the Deep South and the Wild West – Uncle Tom's Cabin and Buffalo Bill. When he was ill with measles, his father gave him a book called *From Peru to San Francisco on Horseback*. In later years, he recalled how this book stimulated his childish imagination:

'I devoured it omnivorously, travelling every inch of the way on the very pommel of the daring rider. On we went through Mexico, Southern Colorado, Arizona, California, on to the North of the United States. I feel certain that this little act of my father caused more rapidly to develop any romantic characteristics which were my heritage and which have manifested themselves in my compositions. . . . I might with truth acknowledge that the songs I ultimately wrote for Eugene Stratton were, as far as their subjects were concerned, given birth to in the course of these imaginary travels.'

When he was eight, the family moved to Manchester. His father bought a house in Blossom Street, Ancoats, and started a cabinet-making business. He bought a piano, for no better reason than to show the neighbours that the Barretts were doing very nicely. As none of the family could play a note, young Tom was packed off to learn how to play it.

His father was a regular patron at the Slip Inn, off Market Street, where the landlord had followed the London fashion and converted his upstairs room into a 'music-hall' for Saturday night entertainment. Music-hall was then a relatively new idea: but every publican soon saw the opportunity for building up his trade by expanding his premises, and adding a room for entertainment. The more ambitious took over the building next door: so, in London, the famous Weston's Music-Hall (later the Holborn Empire) was constructed out of a school, the South London from a chapel, and the London Pavilion from a stable-yard. In Manchester, at the Slip Inn, Tom Barrett was introduced to music-hall in an appropriately dramatic fashion, when the pianist dropped dead at the keyboard, and young Tom was dragged out of bed to take his place. He was twelve at the time.

His brother Steve was an amateur singer: and it was he who encouraged Tom to try his hand at composition. One of the first songs he wrote was dedicated to the landlord of the Slip Inn – Mr O'Riley.

> *Master O'Riley has come back to town,*
> *Go and see the great O'Riley.*
> *Ev'ry one said, 'Thought he was dead'.*

13

But no, not a bit is he, very much fit is he.
I think he's an old Rip van Winkle,
Is O'Riley, Rip O'Riley –
All the town is upside down;
They're all coming over
to say to the rover:

Is that you O'Riley,
Of whom we've heard tell?
Is that the O'Riley
Who keeps the hotel?
If that's the O'Riley
That's talked of so highly.
Well, really, O'Riley
You are looking so well!

The patrons of the early music-hall were a rough and boozy lot: and it was certainly no place for a respectable young man to earn a living. When he was fourteen, Tom Barrett applied for the post of organist at the Roman Catholic Cathedral in Salford, near Manchester. But his reputation as a popular songwriter was no recommendation to the Bishop of Salford, who would only give him the job provided that he adopt a pseudonym for his music-hall persona, and so protect the church from embarrassment by association. So, on posters and sheet music covers, Tom Barrett became – for a short time – Lester Thomas, and, finally, Leslie Stuart. Under this name he wrote 'Cherished Vows', 'Rip van Winkle', 'Were I a King' and 'The Little Mad'moiselle'.

In the 1890s, songs by Leslie Stuart were beginning to be heard in London. He had found a publisher, and made his mark with one or two singers who were happy to use his material. To be adopted by a top-line artist was the ambition of every young songwriter: a picture of Marie Lloyd, Gus Elen, or Albert Chevalier on the songcover was a guarantee of the song getting a good hearing. This was not always to the writer's *financial* advantage: in the early days of song publishing, it was common practice for a singer to buy a song outright for a guinea, thereby depriving the songwriter of any future royalties.

In 1892, Lottie Collins exploded onto the stage of the Oxford Music-Hall, with a song recently imported from America, 'Ta-ra-ra Boom-de-ay!' A journalist of the day, Frank Rutter, described Lottie Collins singing 'this barbaric hymn as if in a trance, to an audience as still and serious as if it was in a church: and then throwing herself into her "abandon dance", which would be encored until she was exhausted'.

The Slip Inn, Manchester, scene of Leslie
Stuart's first introduction to music-hall

For the next four years, this song affected the country 'like an epidemic'. The wild, nonsense chorus (easy to memorise) became 'the theme song of a generation bent on kicking over the traces'. It spawned parodies of itself in music-hall and theatre: infected by this mood of frivolity, Leslie Stuart wrote 'The Girl on the Ran-Dan-Dan', and Lottie Collins sang it:

The dancing in society
Is rather free, but you'll agree
A lady should dance like a lady.
The dreamy waltz goes rather flat
With 'pas de quatre' and such as that,
Though etiquette professes, as everybody knows
To keep a proper level for the toes,
But up went mine at the ball the other night –
Mama was in a fright
Said 'What an awful sight!'
And oh, how she cried when I said 'I'm not to blame –
Why, the girl who sang 'Ta-ra-ra' did the same!'

In the 1890s, Leslie Stuart was successfully combining three careers – songwriter, church organist and impresario. Inspired by the great Sir Charles Hallé, whose concerts at Manchester's Free Trade Hall he attended as a child, he now launched a series of classical music concerts at the St James' Hall: 'Thomas A. Barrett's Popular Concerts', with leading soloists of the day like Patti and Paderewski, and a large orchestra and chorus trained and conducted by himself. He loved the music of Beethoven and Bach. How he reconciled this homage with his other, ruder, passion, is difficult to imagine. It's quite a leap from the Olympian heights of Beethoven's Choral Symphony to the promenade of the Oxford Music-Hall, where, in W. L. George's words, 'from the moment when the conductor, in his elaborately luxurious and irredeemably faulty dress suit, addresses his first and infinitely disabused bow to the audience, to the time when he calls upon the band to produce the smallest possible scrap of "God Save the Queen", there is no flagging. . . . The main thing is the band, the harsh rapid band, that never stops, that plays anything, providing it is the thing of the day, with all the regularity and indifference of the typewriter. From it gush patriotism, comedy or sentiment, and all three burst forth with their full headline value. There is no tickling of big drums; when the drum is banged you know it; nor is there measure in the sigh of the oboe, for the music hall paints not in wash-greens and grays; scarlet, black, white and electric-blue are its gamut.'

But there were changes in the air. In 1896, the magazine *Home Notes* declared: 'Time was when music-hall songs were decried as being vulgar, low, and commonplace. All this is now being considerably altered. Composers for the music-hall are beginning to write *genuine music*. Mr Leslie Stuart stands first in this movement.'

At the Alhambra, the 'Sisters Hawthorne' – an American trio – sang Leslie Stuart's 'The Willow Pattern Plate' in Chinese costumes, in front of a huge circular backdrop. And at the Tivoli, the great Vesta Tilley sang a new song which Stuart had written for his eldest daughter, 'Sweetheart May'. W. R. Titterton describes the scene:

'A dapper young man in an exquisite purple holiday costume strolls from the wings leaning on his bending cane. He comes to the centre of the footlights, and poses with crossed legs and staring monocle, the features deliciously quizzical and inane. A perfect picture . . . the picture speaks and the illusion is piquantly broken, or, rather, the optical illusion continues, only there is another person present – the woman artist who unfolds the tale . . . every gesture is right; every tone is right – striking the delicate chord between irony and burlesque. . . . How sure the singer is! How despotically she rules over her audience – dallies with the rhythm, draws it out – pauses in mid-gesture, the hand in the air, the monocle nearing the eye – pauses so perilously long you get uneasy. . . .'

In 1896, Leslie Stuart gave up his double life. He left the organ loft, cancelled his Saturday concerts and came to live in London. He bought a large house overlooking Battersea Park, where he installed his wife, Kitty, their five children, and the ancient harmonium on which he wrote his songs. What finally provoked him to make this momentous decision, to kill off Thomas A. Barrett, and renounce Beethoven and Bach, nobody knows. Perhaps he was no longer ashamed of calling himself a songwriter, or admitting to his love of music-hall. He was in good company: led by the Prince of Wales, a new audience from the middle and upper classes was beginning to discover the delights of music-hall. The painter, Walter Sickert, was obsessed with the colours and contrasts of the scene. He described what he saw in a letter to a friend:

'A graceful girl leaning forward from the stage, to accentuate the refrain of one of the sentimental ballads so dear to the frequenters of the halls, evoked a spontaneous movement of sympathy and attention in an audience whose sombre tones threw into more brilliant relief the animated movement of the singer, bathed as she was in a ray of green limelight from the centre of the roof, and from below in the yellow radiance of the footlights. . . .'

Max Beerbohm came down from Oxford, to sit with a fellow-undergraduate in the stalls of the Tivoli: 'Lordly aloof, both of us, from the joyous vulgarity of our environment, we would talk in undertones about Hesiod and Fra Angelico, about the lyric element in Marcus Aurelius and the ethics of apostasy as illustrated by the Oxford Movement.

'Though our intellects may not have been so monstrous fine as we pretended, we were quite honest in so far as neither of us could have snatched any surreptitious pleasure in the entertainment as such. We came simply that we might bask in the glow of our own superiority – superiority not only to the guffawing clowns and jades around us, but also to the cloistered pedascules who, no more exquisite than we in erudition, were not in touch with modern life and would have been scared like so many owls, in that garish temple of modernity, a Music Hall, wherein we, on the other hand, were able to sit without blinking. Were we, after all, so very absurd?'

In 1897, London celebrated Queen Victoria's Diamond Jubilee. In the wave of patriotic fervour that accompanied the celebrations, a Leslie Stuart song – 'The Soldiers of the Queen' – became the anthem for the Jubilee. The song cost Leslie Stuart a forty-shilling fine at Marlborough Street Court, on the charge of assaulting a street-trader who tried to sell him a pirated copy of his own song, for a penny. Infuriated by the double indignity of this episode, Stuart declared war against the musical pirates who were then churning out illegal copies of every song that caught the public fancy. A loophole in the copyright laws made prosecution impossible: so Stuart lobbied with his fellow-composers for a change in the law which, some years later, they were able to secure. He also became a founder-member of the Performing Rights Society.

Established in Battersea, Stuart became a regular patron of the London music-halls – the Royal Holborn, The Middlesex, The 'Troc'. It was at the Oxford that he was first introduced to the American singer, Eugene Stratton. Stratton had come to England with Haverly's Minstrel Show, one of several black-face troupes that invaded London in the second half of the nineteenth century: The Christy Minstrels; The Ethiopian Serenaders; McNish, Johnson and Slavin's Refined Minstrels; The Mohawks. The Minstrel companies played in concert halls, like the St James's in Piccadilly, or the Islington Agricultural Hall. They provided what was considered to be a far more decorous form of entertainment than the music-hall, suitable for family audiences and Sunday outings. Their sentimental, nostalgic ballads evoked

Vesta Tilley in character as the
'dapper young man in exquisite costume'

The Gallery at the Old Bedford Music-Hall
in its Edwardian heyday, as painted by Sickert

an imaginary world of tranquillity and order, that was immensely appealing to Victorian audiences. For a time it seemed that England was 'divided into two classes, those who wanted to become minstrels and those who did not'.

When Haverly's Minstrels went home to America, Eugene Stratton stayed behind. He tried to establish himself as a solo singer in music-hall – at first, with a white face. This met with little success, so he blacked up again and became a 'coon delineator'. It was in this guise that Leslie Stuart first saw him, and was so impressed that he wrote a song especially for him:

20

Oh! Is yer mammie always with ye,
  Susie, Susie Ann?
Won't ye come away to hear what a
  wants for to tole ye?
Won't you try to slip de lady, surely
  Sue, ye can?
Is yer mammie always with ye, is she
  with ye now, ma Susie Ann?

Eugene Stratton was not a particularly good singer – his voice had little range or resonance. But he knew all there was to know about how to *sing* a song: he *acted* it rather than sang it, he put it over with such conviction that the story came alive. He performed without the rolling eyes and waving hands of the 'Uncle Tom' minstrel – as adopted by Al Jolson, twenty-five years later. In Stratton's characterisation, the singing negro was a gentle, wistful romantic who sung from the heart, and danced 'like a spirit of the air, with perfect grace and rhythm'.

For Leslie Stuart, this extraordinary figure became the absolute incarnation of his childhood fantasies. He created a whole series of 'song scenes' for Stratton, and they became the talk of the town. From the *Pall Mall Gazette*: 'Mr Leslie Stuart's "Cake Walk" was an immediate success when presented for the first time at the Oxford Music-Hall on Monday night. Eugene Stratton sings and dances with his usual quaintness and ease. Then a very large black lady appears, followed by other coons and coonesses: Eugene processes and goes through the evolution of the cake-walk to an ear-haunting tune.' The 'Coon Drum Major' caused a sensation, when twenty-four black-faced soldiers in scarlet uniforms marched onto the stage behind Eugene Stratton. (It cost Stuart twenty-four half-crowns to persuade some guardsmen from Knightsbridge Barracks to black up for the evening.)

As the Stuart and Stratton partnership strove for new dramatic effects, the staging of the songs became more and more elaborate. In 'The Banshee', Stratton played the part of a coloured boy shipwrecked on the shores of Donegal, where the local people believed him to be a fairy. In 'I May be Crazy', he became a negro horse thief on the run for his life with the posse on his heels: but still the hunted man has to see his girl for the last time. The song ended with a mad violent dance of 'abandon' – all the more grim for its silence. 'As the posse drag him away,' wrote W. Macqueen-Pope, 'he wrenches round in their grasp to give one last despairing glance of dumb, stricken grief at the house of his loved one, and throw out his arms in a mute appeal. . . .'

Eugene Stratton, as man-about-town

The music for 'I May be Crazy' is a perfect piece of dramatic scoring. This is songwriting on a different plane from the verse/chorus repetition of the early music-hall songs. Like film music, which synchronises with every change of scene, Stuart underlines every detail in the story with a musical effect. It's almost as if he carried in his head a picture of Stratton performing the song, and wrote an accompaniment to fit. This remarkable affinity between writer and performer was soon picked up by

Eugene Stratton, as 'coon delineator'

the sensitive antennae of the music-hall audience: devotees flocked to the Oxford Music-Hall, where the first performance of a new Leslie Stuart song became an event – even warranting a special review in *The Times*. Eugene Stratton now acquired the sobriquet 'Idol of the Halls', and put his fee up to £200 a week. Leslie Stuart sold his house in Battersea, and moved to Hampstead.

23

In 1899, the magazine *Answers* announced: 'Mr Leslie Stuart, who came to London three years ago, and began to write the coon songs which have brought him so much fame and fortune, is meditating producing a comic opera very shortly. . . .'

Looking beyond the Oxford Music-Hall, Leslie Stuart now set his sights on the Gaiety Theatre in the Strand, where George Edwardes had launched a new form of entertainment, which became known as musical comedy. A melodious score, a light-hearted and inconsequential plot – the whole confection admirably suited to an after-dinner audience who only wanted to hear a song, or see a dance, or stare at a pretty chorus-girl. George Edwardes – known as the 'Guv'nor' – had brought together a talented team of authors, composers and lyric-writers to create these high-class entertainments, which seemed so perfectly to match the mood of the times. 'It is no use trying to judge the Gaiety by rational standards', wrote *The Times*'s music critic. 'Only go prepared to surrender to her frivolity, and in a few minutes it is ten to one that your eye will be glued to her kaleidoscope, to be moved very rarely.'

In a Gaiety production, any connection between the songs and the story was considered immaterial. If Edwardes liked a song, he put it in, and Leslie Stuart songs had been injected into shows like *The Shop Girl*, *An Artist's Model* and *The Yashmak*. Then, in 1899, Stuart was invited to write a complete score for a musical comedy. Set in the South Seas, it was called *Florodora*. The story was written by Owen Hall, and the plot – such as it was – centred on a perfume, called 'Florodora', which was manufactured on a Philippine Island. An orphan girl owns the perfume: a wicked magnate tries to steal it away from her.

Florodora opened at the Lyric Theatre on 1 November 1899. It was still running when Queen Victoria died, and it ran on into the reign of King Edward, who had seen it many times as Prince of Wales. The song that stopped the show every night was an elaborate production number – a 'double sextette', sung by six pretty girls in long skirts with parasols and six top-hatted and frock-coated admirers, declaring their emotions on bended knee:

> 'Tell me pretty maiden, are there
>   any more at home like you?'
> 'There are a few, kind sir, but
>   simple girls, and proper too.'
> 'Then, tell me, pretty maiden, what
>   these very simple girlies do?'
> 'Kind sir, their manners are perfection,

The 'double sextette' from *Florodora*,
as it was performed at the Lyric Theatre

> *and the opposite of mine.'*
> *'Then take a little walk with me, and*
> *then I can see, what a most*
> *particular girl should be.'*
> *'I may love you too well to let you go*
> *and flirt with those at home, you know.'*

Leslie Stuart made a fortune out of *Florodora*. During his lifetime the royalties exceeded £35,000: and for fifty years after his death, 'Tell me, Pretty Maiden' continued to accumulate royalties for his estate. Stuart spent his fortune lavishly. He added a billiard room and a winter garden to his home in Hampstead. He bought furniture, pictures, jewellery. He was a frequent visitor, with his friend Eugene Stratton, to Hurst Park racecourse. Cricket was another passion: he loved to entertain visiting teams from overseas. He took up croquet, and was soon organising midnight competitions with a candle on every hoop.

His fame was now spreading across the Atlantic: *Florodora* was one of the first musicals by an English composer to be produced on Broadway. It opened at the Casino Theatre in New York in 1900, with the composer himself conducting the orchestra in the pit. From New York, they toured America with sensational success. The impact of *Florodora* on American popular music finds a contemporary witness in the ninety-four-year-old negro pianist Eubie Blake – composer of 'Memories of You'

and 'I'm just wild about Harry'. He saw the original American production of *Florodora*, and heard the score conducted by Leslie Stuart
himself at the Ford Theatre in Baltimore, his home town.

'I said to myself "If only I could write tunes like that": I couldn't write
music then. But I started to write melodies from that day. That man, that
Leslie Stuart, I love him in his grave. He is the cause, the *direct cause* of
me becoming a composer.'

Meanwhile, on the other side of the Atlantic, Eugene Stratton was
trying out a new Leslie Stuart song at the Oxford Music-Hall. For the
first time in their long creative association, Leslie Stuart was not
present to hear the first performance. Ironical too, because it was the
song by which they are both remembered to this day – 'The Lily of
Laguna'. While Stratton was drifting across the stage of the Oxford 'like
thistledown', singing of his negro shepherdess, Leslie Stuart was conducting the overture for *Florodora* in New Orleans. It would be nice to
imagine that he was in Laguna on that night – in fact, he wasn't very far
away. Although he never visited Laguna, he knew where it was. 'If
you're going from New Orleans to California', he told a friend, 'it lies a
matter of a hundred miles on your left.'

His return to London coincided with the end of the Boer war. He
promptly wrote a new topical song for *Florodora*:

> *There came a cry 'To arms!'*
> *The frock-coat lost its charm*
> *And so the topper came a cropper,*
> *At the rat-a-plan.*
> *You lose a lot of chances,*
> *And you don't get asked to dances,*
> *If you're not dressed all in khaki*
> *Like a military man.*
>
> *I want to join the military,*
> *I've got no chance with Jane or Flo*
>   *or Mary*
> *I want to hear the martial rat-a-plan*
> *I want to be a military man.*

He wrote more musical comedies – *The Silver Slipper, The Schoolgirl,
The Belle of Mayfair*. Whatever the setting, he always managed to work
in one of his favourite minstrel ballads. So, in *The Schoolgirl*, set in a
convent, Billie Burke sang of the pleasures of canoeing in the Yukon.
And in the *The Belle of Mayfair* a society drawing-room was the setting

Camille Clifford: the aloof eroticism
of the quintessential Gibson Girl

for the song 'In Montezuma'. If anyone dared to ask, 'Why Red Indians in Mayfair?' Stuart's answer was always, 'Why not?' *The Belle of Mayfair* opened simultaneously in London and New York. An American singer, Camille Clifford, created a sensation in the show as the living embodiment of The Gibson Girl – an ideal beauty as characterised by the American artist Charles Dana Gibson – tiny waist, shapely figure, low-cut dress.

In *The Belle of Mayfair* the two loves of Leslie Stuart's life rubbed shoulders for the last time: the aloof eroticism of the Gibson Girl, and the music-hall simplicity of Billie Burke. Styles were changing: music-hall and musical comedy were on the wane, revue and ragtime were on the horizon.

Leslie Stuart moved out of London. He bought a house on the river and spent more time at the races than at the piano. He quarrelled with Eugene Stratton at Hurst Park, and never wrote another song for him. His supremacy in the musical theatre was now being challenged by new composers – Lionel Monckton, Ivan Caryll, Franz Léhar. Leslie Stuart had his last big London success with *Peggy* in 1908: his next two shows flopped – *The Slim Princess* never even got as far as a London opening. When war broke out, he was bankrupt. To try and recover his losses, he took to the stage again – but this time as an accompanist, playing the piano, while his daughter, May, sang a selection of Leslie Stuart songs. They opened at Golders Green Hippodrome: their fee was £125 a week.

In 1915, *Florodora* was revived at the Lyric; and in 1920 a new production opened in New York. Stuart went to New York with the show, taking with him the score of his most ambitious project ever – which he had been secretly working on for many years – an opera, called *Nina*. An American producer agreed to stage it and Stuart stayed in New York to put the finishing touches to the score. He became friendly with a young dancer called Rudolph Valentino, and promised him a part in *Nina*: in fact, he wrote a tango specially for him. He drew the line at letting him sing, although there was a number in the show called 'Neapolitana' that Valentino was very keen to try. Sadly, even before the start of rehearsals, Stuart quarrelled with his American producers and walked out, taking his *Nina* with him. Back in England, nobody would touch it; and even to this day it remains unpublished, unknown, unperformed.

In the 1920s, when jazz and syncopation were the thing, there was no place for the delicate, sentimental ballads of Leslie Stuart. He wrote a song in protest at the American invasion that was taking place in popular music.

Series 2417

Mr. Farren Soutar.   Miss Camille Clifford.   Miss Billie Burke.
THE HARLEQUINADE IN THE BELLE OF MAYFAIR.

Davidson Brothers
LONDON

The Belle of Mayfair: Camille Clifford in Pompadour wig
stands in contrast to Billie Burke's more ingenuous style

> *What's goin' to happen when the*
>   *ragtime's gone?*
> *Give it a name for I don't know:*
> *All the folks around the Universe*
>   *couldn't be worse*
> *On ragtime – they've a 'hangover'*
>   *jag time:*
> *What's goin' to happen when we all*
>   *sing straight,*
> *Singin' in reason and in rhyme?*
> *What's the matter with the good*
>   *old way?*
> *Never syncopate in what we say,*
> *Never talking like a ragtime melody*
> *That's out of tune – that's out of*
>   *time. . . .*

In 1926, a big revue was staged at the London Palladium. The stars

29

were Billy Merson, George Clarke and Anton Dolin. Just before the interval, the curtain rose on an elderly, silver-haired, sad-looking man, sitting alone at a grand piano. 'His strong mouth was closed in a firm line, his eyes gazed far away as if oblivious of his surroundings,' remembered W. Macqueen-Pope. 'Then quite softly, he began to play. The audience grew still, and listened as, from his skilful fingers, came the strains of songs he had given the world – songs that audience had known and remembered since childhood. Many of them had never seen him before, but they knew his songs. He wove a spell around them, and that great audience began to nod and move in time to the music. And then – it began to sing. The man at the piano played on and on, seemingly unconscious of the ever-growing excitement and enthusiasm around him as one well-beloved melody followed on another. Leslie Stuart, as he sat there playing, must have seen his whole life pass in review before him, as that vast crowd began to cheer and acclaim him.'

He died two years later. *The Manchester Guardian* paid this tribute to him: 'From the Boer War almost to the end of the Great War, any average company to whom music in its higher flights was a mystery, might be depended on to join with affection in the comparative intricacies of "Tell Me, Pretty Maiden" or follow with devotion the neat and gay modulations of "The Lily of Laguna". True, the triumph was not won with Stuart's best weapons, for it needed the commonplace boastfulness of "The Soldiers of the Queen" to bring him the tribute of the complacent England that liked nothing better than music-hall heroics about its little red-coated army. But he atoned notably in the scores that followed, and to hear *Florodora* today is to find an oasis in a desert of percussion and syncopation, and to remember him with gratitude.'

Leslie Stuart rehearsing some of his songs
with his daughter May

LIONEL MONCKTON

'Arcady is
Ever Young'

On 28 April 1909 London play-goers flocked to the Shaftesbury Theatre for the opening of a new musical show, produced by Robert Courtneidge (his seventeen-year-old daughter, Cicely, was in the chorus). *The Arcadians* was billed as a 'Fantastic Musical Play'; when the curtain rose, the audience found itself transported to a fairytale world – a world far removed from the grey urban landscape of the new century.

> *Far away in Arcady*
> *Summer never passes,*
> *Warm the wind that wanders free*
> *Thro' the bending grasses;*
> *Sunbeams peeping thro' the shade*
> *Mint a golden treasure;*
> *Dimpled youth goes down the glade*
> *Hand in hand with Pleasure!*
> *Land of love and land of mirth,*
> *Land where peace and joy had birth,*
> *There the birds have ever sung:*
> *Arcady, Arcady is always young!*

This was Lionel Monckton's vision of Arcadia. With his collaborators Howard Talbot and Arthur Wimperis, he conjured up a peaceful, rustic fairyland, inhabited by artless nymphs and shepherds who try, but fail, to convert the restless Edwardians to their simple way of life.

The Arcadians represents musical comedy's 'coming of age'. This is one of the first truly *integrated* English musicals: the songs are not just

33

An unknown Gaiety Girl and (*right*) 'Stage-Door Johnnies' photographed outside the stage door of the old Gaiety

tuneful interludes – they serve to advance the story, and develop the characters. It's a far cry from the plotless, frivolous variety shows produced by George Edwardes at the Gaiety Theatre, where Lionel Monckton had his first encounter with musical comedy, and fell under the spell of the Gaiety Girls:

> *Now gather girls from near and far*
> *wherever you may be,*
> *I never care how close you are,*
> *So don't mind squeezing me.*
> *I feel that life is full of charm if*
> *I can live like this –*
> *A girl or two on either arm,*
> *and all the rest to kiss!*

When he took over the Gaiety Theatre in 1886, George Edwardes had inherited some sound advice from his predecessor, John Hollingshead: 'A Manager should never forget that there are in London many gentlemen, old and young, who will go to the theatre to admire the beauty of the female actresses.' Edwardes accordingly filled his chorus line

with the loveliest girls he could find, regardless of their ability to sing or dance.

The audience never complained that the Gaiety Girls *did* very little, except parade around the stage looking beautiful. Max Beerbohm noted: 'The look of total surprise that overspreads the faces of these ladies whenever they saunter on to the stage and behold us for the first time, making us feel that we have taken rather a liberty in being there: the faintly cordial look that appears for an instant in the eyes of one of them who happens to see a friend among us, . . . the splendid non-chalance of these queens, all so proud, so fatigued, all seeming to wonder why they were born, and born to be so beautiful. . . .'

Every night, the Gaiety Stage door was besieged by their admirers. The Maharajah of Cooch Behar came nightly through the fog to pay court to Miss Edna May 'with a cluster of jewels on his great white turban, and his hands full of gems'. The Sultan of Zanzibar wanted to buy Madge Saunders, but George Edwardes pointed out the special clause in the Gaiety contract, which expressly prevented any girl from leaving during the run of a show 'for matrimonial reasons'. It was a sensible precaution: the Gaiety Girls had access to Ascot, Goodwood,

the best restaurants and the grandest houses in London – it was but a short step from there to a rich marriage or, failing that, a rewarding breach-of-promise action. Rosie Boot and Denise Orme were among the first to win their tiaras, while Birdie Sutherland had to be content with £10,000 to assuage her wounded pride. Lord Orkney declared: 'If I were ever to lose my wife, I should go and sit on the steps of the Gaiety stage door and marry the next girl who came out of it.' A Gaiety comedian, George Grossmith, described the Gaiety stage door as 'one of the minor wonders of the world . . . The favour of Jupp, the stage door keeper, was a thing not lightly sought, or easily won. I have seen Royal princes, *but not princes of the blood*, being refused admission.'

Lionel Monckton had all the right credentials to enter this select fraternity. His father was Sir John Monckton, Town Clerk of the City of London; his mother was a distinguished actress. Young Lionel had been educated at Charterhouse and Oriel College, Oxford, where he wrote songs for the University Dramatic Society, and the 'Philo-thespians'. His parents wanted him to study law: and in 1885 he was called to the bar. He became a member of Lincoln's Inn, and even held a brief for Lord Alfred Douglas in the Oscar Wilde case. But another side of him was simply stage-struck; and, in order to gain an entrée to the world of the musical theatre, he became a critic – first for the *Pall Mall Gazette*, and later for the *Daily Telegraph*. It was as a theatre critic that he had his first encounter with the 'Guv'nor' of the Gaiety, George Edwardes, who knew of Monckton's interest in songwriting and, typically, invited him to submit some of his songs for the new Gaiety production *The Shop Girl*. That Monckton's songs might not suit the *story* of the show was, as usual, of little concern to Edwardes: if he liked a song, he put it in. So *The Shop Girl*, which opened in November 1894, included a minstrel song by Leslie Stuart ('Louisiana Lou'), a suggestive music-hall song by the American composer Felix McGlennon ('And Her Golden Hair was Hanging Down Her Back'), and a new Chorus for the Gaiety Girls by Lionel Monckton.

In the wings of the Gaiety, Lionel Monckton gave the impression of being a 'fish out of water'. Although he cut a fine figure in a tail-coat, he couldn't emulate the style and panache of the 'crutch and toothpick' brigade – the young 'mashers' who congregated nightly in the stalls, wielding their crutch-sticks and sucking on their gold toothpicks as they ogled Edwardes's latest discoveries. Alongside them, the sombre, balding figure of Lionel Monckton seemed to be in another world. He was often observed standing near the pit or the gallery doors with a

The much-photographed Gaiety Girls:
an anonymous collector's choice

The rise of a Gaiety Girl:
Rosie Boote in stage costume

little counting machine in his pocket, on which he kept a tally of the number of people who came in for matinées or evening performances.

The *Daily Chronicle* reviewed the opening night of *The Shop Girl*: 'The performance was a triumph for all concerned. Mr Caryll has supplied some exceedingly pretty and graceful music, although in point of popularity, it may be questioned whether Mr Lionel Monckton's contributions do not carry off the palm.'

The Shop Girl ran for 546 performances at the Gaiety. In its wake came a whole series of shows with 'girl' titles – all with songs by Lionel Monckton. For *The Circus Girl* he wrote 'A Little Bit of String' for Ellaline Terriss: and for *A Runaway Girl* he produced a new song, which came to him while he was held up in Boulogne by a thunderstorm. He seemed to find loud noises a positive aid to composition: 'I find the roar of the traffic, the whirl of a train, the hum of a motor-car often useful. But a barrel-organ is fatal.' Monckton's 'Thunderstorm' song turned out to be his most durable popular hit, 'Soldiers in the Park'.

The Prince of Wales came to see *A Runaway Girl* at the Gaiety, and

Rosie Boote in her non-theatrical
role as Marchioness of Headfort

joined with the rest of the audience (who could resist?) in singing
Monckton's rousing chorus. But the Royal party took offence at
another Monckton song, 'I Love Society'. When Connie Ediss sang the
lines:

> *I'd ride on horses with fine long tails*
> *If my Papa was Prince of Wales. . .*

His Royal Highness was seen to turn his back on the stage. Apologies
had to be sent to Buckingham Palace.

Despite this moment of lèse-majesté, *A Runaway Girl* proved to be
another runaway success for Edwardes. It also forced Monckton into
taking the plunge, and devoting himself full-time to the musical theatre.
Like other popular composers, before and since, he seems to have been
reluctant at first to take his songwriting seriously. A lover of Wagner,
music critic on the *Daily Telegraph*, described as a 'walking ency-
clopaedia' by his nephews and nieces, perhaps he thought it beneath
his dignity to acknowledge this particular skill, and admit to being the

composer of the catchy tunes that were now being played all over London by German bands, Palm Court orchestras – and even on his hated barrel-organs. The critics were aware of his dilemma:

'However popular and catchy his tunes might be – and they are that, as a matter of course – they are never banal or vulgar. Regret is occasionally expressed by those who admire his accomplished work that it is not associated with productions of a higher order. . . .' Or, on the other hand: 'Here is yet another example of a highly-accomplished musician devoting himself to music of the lightest kind best suited to his powers. . . .'

In 1900, Lionel Monckton collaborated with Ivan Caryll on a complete score for Edwardes's new musical comedy *The Messenger Boy*. As well as the Gaiety production, it was also sent out to Bradford, in one of the many touring companies that were reproducing London shows in the provinces. There could be up to three different versions of the one show 'on the road' at the same time, from the No. 1 company which played at the big city Empires, right down to the No. 3 company at the Temperance Hall or Corn Exchange.

In Bradford, *The Messenger Boy* was playing at the Theatre Royal: and Lionel Monckton travelled north to see it – and to hear his new song 'Maisie', sung by a local girl, Miss Gertie Millar:

> *Maisie is a daisy*
> *Maisie is a dear;*
> *For the boys are mad about her,*
> *And they can't get on without her,*
> *And they all cry 'whoops' when*
> *Maisie's coming near.*
> *Maisie doesn't mind it,*
> *Maisie lets them stare*
> *Other girls are so uncertain*
> *When they do a bit of flirting,*
> *But Maisie gets right there.*

Like everyone else in the audience, Lionel Monckton fell in love with Gertie Millar. He'd never seen anything like her. This was not the cool and withdrawn style of the Gaiety Girls – there was an uninhibited vitality in her performance, a chuckle in her voice, a mischievous look in her eye. And she convinced every member of the audience that she was singing personally, and exclusively, to them.

She was born in Drewton Street, Bradford, in 1880. She made her stage debut, at the age of ten, in a Saturday night concert at the Bradford

The young Gertie Millar

Mechanics' Institute, and then joined Arthur Brogden's 'Swiss Choir'. She played the Principal Girl in pantomime – *Robinson Crusoe* at the Comedy Theatre, Manchester, and *Dick Whittington* at the Prince's, Bradford. Legend has it that she was once a mill girl, and that she wore clogs; but the truth is that, from the age of ten, Gertie Millar sang for her supper.

When he got back to London, Lionel Monckton persuaded George Edwardes to bring Gertie Millar to the Gaiety. He even paid for her to have elocution lessons, to smooth out her Yorkshire vowels. And he started writing songs for her. Gertie Millar made her debut on the Gaiety stage in the summer of 1901 in a show called *The Toreador*.

For the next ten years, Gertie Millar dominated the Gaiety stage, with her slight, reed-like figure, and tiny, breathless voice – 'the words half-spoken and half-sung, so that you had to listen hard to catch their full significance'. From the stalls to the gallery, she was everybody's darling.

Lionel Monckton proposed to Gertie Millar in the wings of the Gaiety, and they were married at St Mark's Church, Surbiton, on 20 December 1902. It was a quiet wedding, which Lady Monckton did not attend. Gertie Millar was 23; her husband – she called him 'Lallie' – was 41. The Gaiety Girls were only slightly envious: after all, Gertie hadn't acquired a title through her marriage – although her reluctant mother-in-law was a Lady.

The following year, to celebrate the recent coronation of his royal namesake, that other fun-loving Edwardian, George Edwardes, opened his *new* Gaiety Theatre on the corner of the Strand and the Aldwych. The old playhouse had been demolished by the LCC as part of a road-widening scheme: in its place rose a fine, green-domed building designed by Ernest Rultz and George Ford in the Florentine style, and topped by a golden girl blowing a trumpet. Opening night was 26 October 1903. The King sent Edwardes a message:

'I've loved the Gaiety, I love you, and I love the Girls. I am bringing Queen Alexandra to the first night.' But they arrived late. The curtain had already gone up on the first act of *The Orchid*, a new musical comedy written by Lionel Monckton, Ivan Caryll and Paul Rubens. W. Macqueen-Pope was in the audience: 'Just as the opening chorus was over, the familiar figure of the King, accompanied by Queen Alexandra, could be seen at the back of the Royal Box. A roar of welcome rang out as their Majesties came forward and took their seats, and so en-thusiastic and prolonged was the cheering that both King and Queen, beaming with delight at the hearty spontaneity of their reception, half rose in their places, and bowed and smiled repeatedly at their loyal subjects.'

The critical response to *The Orchid* was equally enthusiastic. The *Morning Leader* declared: 'It was a good thing to be alive at the new Gaiety last night. It was a splendid, uproarious night – everybody ... waiting only to applaud the old favourites, and help in the launch of a beautiful theatre on a career as famous and successful as that of the old. ... *The Orchid* with its gaiety, high spirits, pretty faces, superb staging and popular tunes, will start on a career of success to which it would be foolhardy to prophesy any term.'

Lionel Monckton's old employer, the *Daily Telegraph*, paid a pretty compliment to his wife: 'Of the younger members of the cast, Miss Gertie Millar distinguished herself most by her exquisite and charming manner, alike as an actress, singer and dancer. Her performance last night brings her into the very front rank of the profession.'

In *The Orchid*, Gertie sang a song for which she had provided the inspiration – and the title. Her husband found her in the bathroom one day, drying her hair in two long plaits, and commented: 'Well! You *do* look a Yorkshire lass.' Gertie replied: 'Yes, I feel a bit of a Liza Ann.' Cue for a song which he wrote there and then:

> *Liza Ann is a neat young lass*
> *And she's working up at Brigg's mill.*
> *Every morning at six o'clock*
> *You can see her walking up the hill.*
> *There she goes with her turned-up nose*
> *And her dinner in a nice tin can.*
> *Oh, you'll all of you be mad,*
>   *when you see another lad,*
> *Is a-taking out Liza Ann!*

A pretty redhead called Ruby Miller made her debut in *The Orchid*, only to be given the sack a week after the opening, when Edwardes discovered that she was only fourteen. Packed off to school again, she promised to return when she grew up.

The Orchid ran for more than two years at the Gaiety; after which it was produced in New York, where English musical comedy was becoming increasingly popular – there being, as yet, no American equivalent. Young composers like Jerome Kern were strongly influenced by these imported European shows: indeed Kern himself was a frequent visitor to Edwardian London, where, with his friend P. G. Wodehouse, he loved to visit the music-halls, and the Gaiety.

A. S. Boyd's drawing of the
opening night of *The Orchid*

After *The Orchid* came *The Cingalee* (with, for the first time, a complete score by Lionel Monckton), *The Spring Chicken*, and *The Girls of Gottenburg*. In 1909, Gertie Millar played the title role in *Our Miss Gibbs* – the story of a shop girl's romance. In the last act she appeared 'wearing a dark blue satin pierrot costume, with white pom-poms and a huge white satin bow under the chin. Eight attendant pierrots in pale blue costumes, a-tumble on the stage, made up the background, though a flutter of ill-fitting gloves should be recalled if the stage picture is to be complete. Then a bewitching little voice made its caressing chant felt through the half-light, and a lithe form moved about the stage like a capful of invigorating wind off a summer sea.'

> *'I'm such a silly when the moon comes out*
> *I hardly seem to know what I'm about;*
> *Skipping, hopping – never, never stopping,*
> *I can't keep still, although I try.*
> *I'm all a-quiver when the moonbeams glance;*
> *That is the moment when I long to dance*
> *I can never close a sleepy eye,*
> *When the moon comes creeping up the sky!'*

Gertie Millar singing 'Moonstruck' is quintessential musical comedy – artless, frivolous, and utterly beguiling. Everyone who saw her was bewitched. At the same time, it's almost impossible to imagine the austere upright figure of her husband actually *writing* the song, or singing those absurd lyrics to himself at the piano. Perhaps Gertie herself had a hand in it.

Meanwhile, her supremacy as queen of the musical stage was facing its first serious challenge. George Edwardes, as always anticipating the public appetite for novelty, had paid £1000 for the rights of a Viennese operetta called *The Merry Widow*: in so doing, he started a fashion that was soon to displace musical comedy almost entirely. In New York, a *Merry Widow* craze swept through the town, leaving in its wake Merry Widow beer cellars, Merry Widow cigars, and Merry Widow corsets. In London, a million people saw *The Merry Widow* at Daly's Theatre, where it ran for nearly 800 performances. Like *The Sound of Music*, in later years, it had its 'freaks'; young Ivor Novello saw the show twenty-seven times, and would have auditioned for a part in the chorus, if his mother had not prevented him. Osbert Sitwell was taken to see the show on an exeat from Eton:

'As the banal, but in a way charming, waltz sounded out, and Miss Lily Elsie

(*Overleaf*) Scene from the original Shaftesbury Theatre production of *The Arcadians*

came down the stairs to her prince, ... I can recall wondering whether it were possible that in the future such entertainments or such an audience would – or could – be considered as being typical of their epoch, or providing a clue to it, in the same way that we looked back, past our fathers, to La Vie Parisienne or Die Fledermaus. I decided, then, that to adopt such a view would be to overrate both entertainment and spectators – but I was wrong. It held a suitably designed mirror to the age, to the preference for restaurant to palace, for comfort to beauty, and to the idealisation of Mammon. Mammon underlay the smudgy softness and superficial prettiness of the whole performance, as the skull supports the lineaments of even the youngest and freshest face.'

In 1909, with a perfect sense of timing, Lionel Monckton composed *The Arcadians*:

> *With a melody enthralling,*
> *Loud the woodland echoes ring.*
> *Hark! the pipes of Pan are calling*
> *With a merry lilt and swing.*
> *Hear their joyous carolling,*
> *Flowing, growing, rising, falling,*
> *Youth and joy must have their fling*
> *When the pipes of Pan are calling – Ah!*
> *The pipes of Pan.*
>
> *So follow, follow, follow,*
> *The merry, merry Pipes of Pan ...*

And they heard the call in their thousands, and came to the Shaftesbury Theatre to share this idealistic vision of a simple, natural world; a vision that found its perfect accompaniment in Monckton's musical score – certainly the best thing he ever wrote.

Sadly, this high-point in his musical career coincided with the breakup of his marriage to Gertie Millar, for whom there was no part in *The Arcadians*. The marriage had been in a fragile state for some years now, as Phyllis le Grand – who used to understudy Gertie Millar – recalls:

'She always disliked me intensely, because *her* men would send me flowers, and chocolates and things, and she thought I was going out with them. But I wasn't allowed – I was brought up like a puritan! Still, if Gertie could snub me in any way, she never missed an opportunity to do it. And this went on until I married. And then after I'd been married about three months, I came down to the theatre to see my husband who was working there. And I was talking to Gertie in the wings, when suddenly she turned to me and said: "You're going to have a

The New Gaiety Theatre in the years
immediately preceding the First World War

49

baby – I know you are – I can tell by your face. Oh, let me stand near you – let me rub against you – they say it's catching – do let me!" She was crazy to have a child, d'you see? And I said to her, "Gertie, why have you never had a baby?" and she said "Well, if you have a uterus up here" – pointing to the top of her spine – "you can't." And if she *had* been able to have a child, they say the Duke of Westminster would have married her. But he was anxious to get an heir, and he couldn't take the chance of marrying a barren woman.'

In 1910, Lionel Monckton wrote his last show for George Edwardes – *The Quaker Girl.* Although he was no longer living with his wife, there were no arguments about who should play the title role. For their friends in the audience, the song 'O, Time, Time!' took on an unbearable poignancy:

> *When a maiden all aglow with expectation*
> *Waits and watches for her lover to appear*
> *In her fanciful and fond imagination*
> *Ev'ry moment seems a year.*
> *All impatient from the break of day till sundown*
> *She keeps wishing that the hours were not so long;*
> *For it seems to her that ev'ry watch has run down,*
> *And that all the clocks are wrong.*

> *O, Time, Time!*
> *You are really most unkind!*
> *Why is it you're inclined*
> *To lag so far behind?*
> *You may go slow*
> *When we meet, my love and I,*
> *But till then I want the time,*
> *I want the time to fly.*

The Quaker Girl was the swansong of traditional musical comedy, in the Gaiety style. The King was dead, and ominous rumblings were beginning to sound all over Europe. From America came new noises and strange rhythms: at the London Hippodrome, 'The American Ragtime Octette' syncopated their way through the new ragtime repertoire, and provoked the theatre's resident conductor to explode: 'This is not music! It is against all the principles of music!'

In the summer of 1914, the Gaiety closed its doors. George Edwardes suffered a stroke and went to Bad Neuheim in Germany to recuperate. He was still there in August, when Britain declared war on Germany. Interned in the Grand Hotel, he suffered a second stroke, and was

Lionel Monckton and
Gertie Millar in happier days

repatriated on a stretcher. He died in October 1915.

Other theatres flourished during the war. Escapism on a grand scale was the order of the day. A costume extravaganza called *Chu Chin Chow* opened at His Majesty's Theatre in 1916, starting a run that was to exceed the duration of the war itself (a record that stood unchallenged for the next 38 years – until *Salad Days*). At Daly's, *The Maid of the Mountains* settled in for four profitable years, with Lottie Collins' daughter Jose playing the title role. One of the songs from *The Maid of the Mountains* seems, in retrospect, to have caught the mood of the day:

'In the 1920s Arcady seemed a long way away.' Denise
Orme (*left*) had become Lady Churston, seen (*right*)
with her son at Eton for the Fourth of June

> *Take no thought for the morrow*
> *Live, just live for today. . . .*

But at the time, the songs that flourished were the jingoistic ballads
and ill-designed recruiting songs:

> *We don't want to lose you,*
> *But we think you ought to go. . . .*

A young cadet in the Naval Air Service – Ivor Novello – was encouraged by his mother to write a patriotic song – which he did, in
twenty minutes. It became the theme song of the Home Front: 'Keep the
Home Fires Burning'.

The poet Siegfried Sassoon expressed the disgust felt by soldiers on leave from the front when they encountered the patriotic fervour, and jolly propaganda, voiced from the safety of a stage in 'Blighty':

> *The house is crammed; tier beyond tier they grin*
> *And cackle at the Show, while prancing ranks*
> *Of harlots shrill the chorus, drunk with din;*
> *'We're sure the Kaiser loves the dear old Tanks!'*
>
> *I'd like to see a Tank come down the stalls,*
> *Lurching to rag-time tunes, or 'Home, Sweet Home' –*
> *And there'd be no more jokes in music-halls*
> *To mock the riddled corpses round Bapaume.*

In 1916, Gertie Millar sang Monckton's 'Chalk Farm to Camberwell Green', in a revue at the Palace called *Bric-à-Brac*. Two years later, she retired. Lionel Monckton complained that theatres were now being run by grocers. He said: 'If people want to mess up music, they can write their own. I'm not going to write any more.'

He was still to be seen at theatrical first nights, pale-faced, wrapped always in a heavy overcoat, and walking with difficulty; looking rather like a retired Army man with his precise grey moustache and somewhat severe manner. He seemd to his friends twenty years older than he really was; but he never allowed his ill-health to interfere with his regular habits, which always included a nightly game of poker at the Green Room Club, and then home to Russell Square, in a horse-drawn cab. He hated motor-cars almost as much as he hated jazz. He died of influenza on 21 February 1924. On the night he died, an apparition appeared at the Green Room Club. His friend, the actor-manager Donald Calthrop, suddenly looked up from the card-table and said, 'I believe something has happened to Lallie. Look – there's his dog.' Monckton often brought his dog, Trixie, to the club, and everybody knew it. His friends looked round, but there was no dog. Later, Calthrop learnt that this visitation had coincided with the moment of Monckton's death.

Another friend, Hartley Carrick, wrote an epitaph, which was printed in *The Referee*:

> *Master of melodies, both old and new,*
> *Now in that realm where all true art belongs,*
> *You'll find the motif that eluded you,*
>   *The Song of Songs.*
> *Master of caustic wit and scathing jest,*

Though there were few who counted you a pal,
We of the fellow-craft, who knew you best,
Shall miss you, Lal.

Shortly after his death, Gertie Millar married into the aristocracy. She became Lady Dudley. In stately homes across the land, ageing Gaiety Girls, who had achieved the final accolade of a title and an estate, were now the only survivors of a Golden Age which was gone forever. In the 1920s, Arcady seemed a long way away.

Land of Love and land of Mirth
Land where peace and joy had birth,
There the birds have ever sung;
Arcady, Arcady, is always young!

NOEL COWARD

'Poor Little Rich Girl'

Noël Coward fell in love with Gertie Millar when he was eleven. With his mother, he used to queue for matinées of Gaiety shows: once, at the stage door, he caught a bouquet which Gertie threw into the crowd of her admirers. The flowers were lovingly preserved for years, pressed between the pages of his *Chums* annual.

He was born in 1899, and lived for the first five years of his life in Waldegrave Road, Teddington. His paternal grandfather was a professor of music and his parents, and all his aunts and uncles (except for Uncle Jim, who played the organ), sang in the choir of St Alban's, Teddington. Of his own introduction to music, he recalled:

'I was born into a generation that still took light music seriously. The lyrics and melodies of operetta, musical comedy, Gilbert and Sullivan were hummed and strummed into my consciousness at an early age. My father sang them, my mother played them, my nurse, Emma, breathed them through her teeth while she was washing me, undressing me, and putting me to bed ... I couldn't help composing tunes even if I wished to, and ever since I was a little boy they have dropped into my mind unbidden – and often in the most unlikely circumstances!'

He made his first public appearance at a school concert when he was six. Dressed in a white sailor suit, he sang a song made famous by Gertie Millar – 'Coo', from *A Country Girl*. He followed this with a song about the spring, for which he accompanied himself on the piano. This feat was acclaimed by the audience, who insisted on an encore. Sadly, the day ended in tears when the young Noël learnt that he was not to be given a prize for his performance.

At the age of eleven, he made his first appearance on the West End stage – in a play for children called *The Goldfish*. In subsequent years, he played a page-boy, a mushroom, and 'Slightly' in *Peter Pan*. He became as stage-struck as his mother, and determined to make a name for himself in the theatre. When he was seventeen, he wrote a song about ambition – 'Forbidden Fruit':

> *Ordinary man invariably sighs*
> *Vainly for what cannot be.*
> *If he's in an orchard he will cast his eyes*
> *Up into the highest tree.*
> *There may be lots of windfalls*
> *Lying all around;*
> *But you'll never see a man enjoy the*
> *   fruit that's on the ground.*
>
> *Every peach out of reach is attractive*
> *'Cos it's just a little bit too high,*
> *And you'll find that every man*
> *Will try to pluck it if he can*
> *As he passes by.*
> *For the brute loves the fruit that's forbidden*
> *And I'll bet you half-a-crown*
> *He'll appreciate the flavour of it*
> *   much, much more*
> *If he has to climb a bit to shake it down.*

In 1920, Noël Coward was living in London: at 111 Ebury Street, next door to a young actress, Edith Evans, with whom he used to walk home at night after the theatre. He was now an established 'juvenile', much in demand for light comedy roles. He'd also become a playwright, and in July appeared in the first of his own plays to be produced in London. *I'll Leave it to You* ran for a modest five weeks at the New Theatre.

He bought his first tail-suit, and, with his friend Gertrude Lawrence, infiltrated the restaurant of the Savoy Hotel (they discovered that it was possible to slip in through the Embankment entrance without paying for a meal). The attraction was not the food but the *music*, as supplied by Bert Ralton, and his New York Havana Band. 'Jazz' had just arrived in London. In 1919, 'The Original Dixieland Jazz Band' astounded audiences at the London Hippodrome and the Hammersmith Palais. Soon every ballroom, restaurant and nightclub had to have its own jazz band – either the real thing, imported from New York, or a local imitation. Noël Coward later described how these new noises and strange rhythms exploded onto the London musical scene:

Florence Mills (*standing*) with chorus in *Dixie to Broadway*

'English composers, taken by surprise and startled by the vital Negro-Jewish rhythms from the New World, fell back in some disorder: conservative musical opinion was shocked and horrified by such alien noises and, instead of saluting the new vitality, turned up its patrician nose and retired disgruntled from the arena.'

But for the young Noël Coward, this American invasion was a positive inspiration. In May 1921, he set sail for the heartland of Jazz – New York – to experience it at first hand. He wrote to his mother: 'This is just a short line to reassure your yearning mother-heart that I am well, considering I had three operations for appendicitis yesterday – was run over by a bus on Tuesday – smitten down by peritonitis on Sunday and am going into consumption tomorrow. But you mustn't worry, because apart from these things, I am *all right*. There are certain to be Icebergs, Hurricanes, Typhoons and Torpedoes but Douglas Fairbanks, I am sure, will save me if you write him a nice letter. By the way, there is a dreadfully dangerous lift in this apartment; several people are killed daily just getting in and out – and the drains are notoriously bad. Diphtheria and Typhoid are inevitable! But *Don't Worry*.'

In New York, he embarked on a frantic round of sightseeing, theatre-going, and socialising. He went to Coney Island, Wall Street, and up to the top of the Woolworth Building. He became friends with Lynn Fontanne and Alfred Lunt, who were 'courting' in a theatrical lodging-house in the West 70s. He went to the Globe Theatre, to see the Ziegfeld Follies 'languidly boring themselves and the audience with their too-perfect figures, their total lack of expression'. He renewed acquaintance with Ronald Colman, who had just opened in a play that was a flop and was on his way to the West Coast to try and get into pictures. He heard Fannie Brice sing 'Secondhand Rose'. He was introduced to Fred Astaire, and saw him dance for the first time, in a musical comedy called *Love Letters*. Every Thursday and Saturday he went to the midnight performances of *Shuffle Along* – the first coloured revue –where he heard the legendary Florence Mills sing 'Bye Bye, Blackbird'. And he went to Harlem, 'drifting from cabaret to cabaret, jigging to alien rhythms and listening to strange wailings and screechings until our feet ached, our ears buzzed, and our eyes blinked in the cool dawn'.

Noël Coward returned from New York, fired with new enthusiasm, and new musical ideas. Looking back on this period, he wrote, 'In my early 20s and 30s it was from America that I gained my greatest impetus. In New York, they have always taken light music seriously. There it is, as it should be, saluted as a specialised form of creative art, and is secure in its own right. . . . Here in England, there are few to write the music, and fewer still to recognise it when it is written. . . .'

On his return to London, Noël Coward set about writing songs and sketches for a new revue to be produced by the celebrated impresario André Charlot. This slick and sophisticated form of theatre had now almost replaced musical comedy on the London stage. The American 'ragtime revue' which set the style had been fused with elements of traditional British seaside concert-party – and even music-hall – to produce an entertainment 'so designed that it doesn't matter how late you get there', according to Ronald Jeans, who was Noël Coward's co-author on the Charlot revue.

In 1922, Noël Coward wrote to his mother, 'I've just played my songs to Charlot and he's delighted. He sat without a smile and then took me aside and said they were *all* good – so that's that. I now quite definitely enter the ranks of British composers. It will be very thrilling to hear all my songs done by a good orchestra, won't it?'

Charlot's new revue opened at the Duke of York Theatre in September 1923. It took its title from the call-sign of the BBC's first broadcasting station – *London Calling*; and the songs that Noël Coward wrote reflected the new attitudes and 'modern' ideas of the day – as well as his

Gertrude Lawrence in costume for 'Parisian Pierrot' in *London Calling*

This Year of Grace: Jessie Matthews and Sonnie Hale in 'A Room with a View' (*above*) and as seen by *The Bystander*'s cartoonist, Macmichael (*right*)

own, newly-acquired, cosmopolitan experience. One song was inspired by a visit to a Berlin nightclub, and the louche cabaret singer who used a Pierrot doll as a prop in her act:

> *Parisian Pierrot,*
> *Society's hero,*
> *The Lord of a day,*

The Rue de la Paix
Is under your sway,
The world may flatter
But what does it matter?
They'll never shatter
Your gloom profound.

'Parisian Pierrot' was the first of Noël Coward's songs to become a popular hit. For the first time, he experienced the thrill of hearing his own music played in restaurants – and of seeing his name in lights outside a theatre. As a performer, however, his highly individual vocal style was not that well received. Some critics even went so far as to suggest that he should never have been allowed to appear in *London Calling* in the first place. Nobody had any such doubts about Gertrude Lawrence, for whom Noël Coward had written several songs – especially 'Carrie':

Carrie as a baby was a darling little pet,
And everybody loved her from the Vicar
   to the Vet.
Her manners when at school were most
   ingenuous and quaint

Lauri Devine miming to 'Dance Little Lady' in *This Year of Grace*

> *She had the reputation of a little*
> *   plaster saint.*
>
> *Carrie was a careful girl,*
> *Such a very careful girl*
> *So far and no further she was quite*
> *   prepared to go,*
> *But still she took precautions 'cos*
> *   of course you never know . . .*

'Carrie' was a perfect child of the 20s. She epitomised the 'New Woman' of the day, cheerfully overturning traditional attitudes to her sex, and breaking out in all directions – smoking and drinking and putting on lipstick in public, cropping her hair, riding in dickie seats, wearing cami-knickers, and reading Marie Stopes.

Noël Coward was fascinated by this 'New Woman' and wrote several of his best songs for, and about, her. In real life, he was equally fascinated by the great and beautiful ladies who dominated the world of theatre, and society, at the time. Gertrude Lawrence had been a close friend ever since they were child actors together. After her came Gladys Cooper, Elsa Maxwell, Diana Cooper, Yvonne Printemps, Marlene Dietrich, and many others. These friendships were described by Noël Coward as 'amitiés amoureuses', which he treasured all his life.

After six months in *London Calling*, Noël Coward set sail once more for his beloved New York. This time he had £250 spending money in contrast to the £17 with which he'd embarked on his first trip. He was now nearly a celebrity: 'My fame, although far from assured, had at least been enough to procure me a dignified pose for the White Star Line photographer at Waterloo, and an enquiry as to my American plans by the press reporter at Southampton.'

He spent a month in New York. *London Calling* opened on Broadway under the title *André Charlot's London Revue of 1924*. Noël Coward wasn't in the cast, and he experienced the mixed pain and pleasure of seeing Jack Buchanan putting over, with great success, songs that had flopped when sung by him in London. He said: 'I could find no adequate reason, except perhaps that it was because he apparently made no effort at all.'

Back in London in the autumn of 1924, he continued working at a furious pace. During these twelve months, he wrote four full-length plays – and played the leading role in one of them, *The Vortex*, which, after a brief skirmish with the Lord Chamberlain, was unveiled before an unsuspecting audience at the Everyman Theatre, Hampstead, in November 1924. It became the talk of the town, and Noël Coward's performance as Nicky Lancaster – hooked on cocaine, betrayed by his adulterous mother – was acclaimed and reviled with equal enthusiasm, by press and public.

Bernard Shaw described the play as 'wonderfully damnable'. Sir Gerald du Maurier said: 'The public are asking for filth – the younger generation are knocking at the door of the dustbin'.

Noël Coward played the leading role in *The Vortex* in four London theatres, one after the other. In April 1925 he was still playing eight performances a week, as well as completing a new play (*Fallen Angels*) and preparing a new revue for C. B. Cochran, *On With The Dance* – for which he wrote book, lyrics *and* music, as well as supervising the auditions and rehearsals. It opened at the London Pavilion – and the hit of the show was a song that Mr Cochran wanted to drop, because he thought it too dreary: 'Poor Little Rich Girl', sung by Alice Delysia.

The critic of the *Morning Post* got rather worked up about *On With The Dance*: 'The speed of the performance is feverish, burlesquing the speed of our modern life. At times the players seem mad, intoxicated with the desire to force their bodies to do something faster and faster. As befits Mr Coward's genius, many of the incidents are as nature seen through a glass crookedly ... the arid, futile people that Mr Coward puts into his plays dash about the stage, worked into a frenzy by the syncopated music.' *The Sketch* printed a photograph of Noël Coward

Bitter-Sweet: (*above*) the duel; (*right*) Peggy Wood
and George Metaxa as seen by Nerman in *The Tatler*

seated at the piano, in a woolly dressing-gown. The caption read 'At home: Our most Daring Playwright'.

With three shows now running in London, Noël Coward once again turned his attention to New York, and by the end of 1926, there were three Noël Coward plays on Broadway. But the strain was telling, and by Christmas – still only twenty-six years old – he was in a state of complete physical and mental exhaustion. 'Melancholia enveloped me like a thick cloud, blotting out the pleasure and colour from everything.'

He decided to get away from it all, and set sail for Sarawak. By the time he reached Honolulu, he was too ill to go any further. He spent the next three weeks on a beach at Mokuleia: thereafter, his therapy for stress and strain was always to put geographical distance between himself and his problems.

He even resisted the temptation to do any work during his Hawaiian convalescence, although a little tune did slip into his mind while he was floating in the surf one day. Nearly a year later, it emerged as 'A Room with a View', which took its place in the 1928 Cochran revue, *This Year of Grace* – sung by Jessie Matthews and Sonnie Hale. For another new Coward song, 'Dance Little Lady', Lauri Devine mimed the part of a modern girl dancing – as Coward himself described it – in that 'lifeless, exhausted, unsmiling fashion that is common among the young who were reared on food-tickets, and bombed into neurosis'.

In the summer of 1928, Noël Coward decided to try his hand at operetta: 'There had been little or no sentiment on the London musical stage for a long while. The operettas at Daly's Theatre, with their crashing second-act finales in which the heroines dissolved in tears, or danced with the footman, had given place to an endless succession of slick American 'Vo-de-o-do' musical farces in which the speed was fast, the action complicated, and the sentimental value negligible. It seemed high time for a little Romantic Renaissance, and very soon a few preliminary melodies began to form in my head.'

The result was *Bitter-Sweet* – a terribly English Viennese operetta which took shape in a car hastily parked on Wimbledon Common, where Coward drafted the story of Sari Linden – a famous singer who elopes

with a penniless songwriter, and, after his death (in a duel), marries into the aristocracy. Another car-ride – this time in a New York taxi – produced the words and music for Sari Linden's 'big number', which also proved to be Noël Coward's most popular and durable song hit: 'I'll See You Again'. It was one of his own favourite compositions.

Bitter-Sweet opened in London in July 1929, and ran for 697 performances at His Majesty's Theatre. It was then produced in New York by the legendary 'Flo' Ziegfeld, who wanted to 'pep up' the chorus line by drafting in twelve of his most ravishing Ziegfeld girls. This offer was firmly rejected by the author, with the result that Ziegfeld, in pique, allowed the show to open in New York without any of the usual bally-hoo. Even so, it was an enormous success, with Evelyn Laye giving the performance of her life as Sari Linden.

The day after the 'Bitter-Sweet' premiere, Noël Coward wrote to his mother: 'There's been a complete disaster on the New York Stock Market; everybody is losing millions, poor old Syrie [Maugham] practically all she had, but it serves them right for gambling. Thank God Jack [Wilson, his business manager] has only invested money in gilt-edged securities and never speculated so I'm perfectly safe, but it really is horrible, people hurling themselves off buildings like confetti.'

Once again, he decided to 'get away from it all', and embarked for Yokohama, via San Francisco and Honolulu. December 1929 found him in Shanghai, with flu. In his bed in the Cathay Hotel, in four days, he wrote *Private Lives*, complete with its unashamedly sentimental theme song 'Someday I'll Find You'.

Private Lives offers a vivid illustration of Coward's much-quoted dictum 'extraordinary how potent cheap music is'. It's *music* that provides the key to Elyot and Amanda's nostalgic reunion: a band playing in the distance prompts their regretful memories of the fun they once had, and the love they had lost. And in Noël Coward's own story, the play takes on an equally potent nostalgic force – almost as if he himself had seen the end of 1929 as a first-act curtain, bringing to a close the decade that he now seems to have adopted as his very own.

To celebrate the end of the Twenties – and his own thirtieth birthday – he devised an epic play, which would chronicle the major events of English history during the years of his own lifetime: from New Year's Eve 1899 to New Year's Eve 1930. This was *Cavalcade*: and, as in *Private Lives*, music was to be the key. The popular melodies of successive generations would be used to evoke the scenes and sensations of the day – as experienced by Noël Coward himself, from childhood to maturity.

Gertrude Lawrence and Noël Coward in
Private Lives at the Phoenix Theatre in 1930

The celebration of Mafeking Night to the strains of Leslie Stuart's 'Soldiers of the Queen' and 'Goodbye, Dolly Gray'. A seaside scene from 1920, with a concert party borrowed from his own memories of 'Uncle George' at Bognor singing 'Put a little bit away for a rainy day'. 'Nearer My God to Thee', played by the ship's orchestra on the deck of the doomed *SS Titanic*. The War, with its jolly recruiting songs 'We don't want to lose you, but we think you ought to go' and 'On Sunday I walk out with a Soldier', which the young Coward heard sung by Gwen Brogden in *The Passing Show* at the Palace; then the scenes at Victoria Station, with hospital trains arriving, leave trains pulling out, 'It's a Long Way to Tipperary' . . . Armistice Night crowds in Trafalgar Square singing 'Land of Hope and Glory'. . . .

Finally, New Year's Eve 1930, in a brassy noisy nightclub: the 'bright young things' in full cry and a song for the times – 'a comment accurate enough and empty enough' – 'Twentieth Century Blues'.

In this strange illusion,
Chaos and confusion,
People seem to lose their way.
What is there to strive for,
Love or keep alive for? Say –
Hey, hey, call it a day.
Blues,
Nothing to win or to lose.
It's getting me down.
Who's
Escaped those dreary
Twentieth Century Blues?

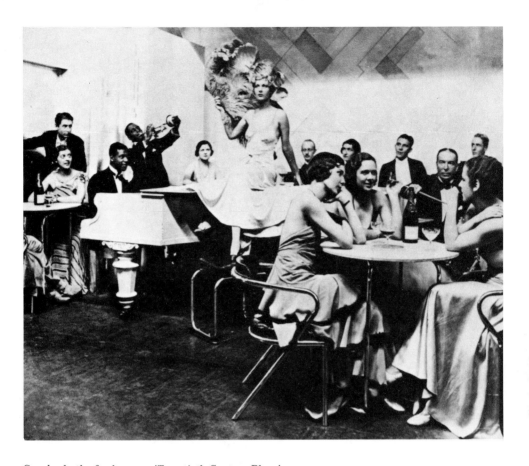

Cavalcade: the final scene – 'Twentieth Century Blues'

A new caricature study of dance maestro Ray Noble by the Toronto artist, Ted Parlane.

Parlane
37.

RAY NOBLE

'Goodnight Sweetheart'

On 25 May 1932, Noël Coward went to the new HMV studios in Abbey Road, to record a medley of his own songs, including 'I'll See You Again', and 'Someday I'll Find You'. He was met there by a skinny young man, with unruly 'sticking-up' hair that made him look even taller than he was, who introduced himself as HMV's Light Music Director, conductor of the house orchestra, and the arranger for the Noël Coward recording. This was Ray Noble – bandleader and songwriter, the man destined to resist the American ragtime invasion, and, single-handed, take his own elegant music into the heart of the enemy camp. In fact, the name of Ray Noble became so identified with American bands, and musicians like Glenn Miller and Tommy Dorsey, that his Englishness was often overlooked.

He was born in Brighton, in 1907. His father was a neurologist: his uncle, Thomas Tertius Noble, played the organ, and was eventually to become the organist of St Thomas's Episcopal Church in Manhattan. Ray Noble studied the piano at the Royal Academy of Music, and seemed destined for a concert-hall career. In later years, he explained how he became side-tracked:

'It must have been in about 1926: I went to a place in Wimbledon – the "Palais de Danse" they called it then. There was a band there, and I heard this fellow playing "Kitten on the Keys", which was I think the first of Zez Confrey's ragtime piano pieces. It was *electrifying* to me. I had to go and climb round the back of the bandstand to see what it was! Then I got a copy of it, locked myself in the front room with the piano, and stayed there all afternoon till I could play it. And I think that really gave me an interest in this kind of music. After that I bought every song copy I could lay my hands on. Then I got together with some other guys – more by accident than anything else – and we started a small group, playing clubs and dances and so forth in South London.'

By 1927, the American musical invasion was well under way. Hotels, clubs, restaurants and dance-halls echoed to the exciting new sounds of Dixieland Jazz and the twelve-bar blues. American musicians in-filtrated the local dance bands – Paul Whiteman, Bunny Berrigan and Abe Lyman vied for popularity with Jack Hylton and Ambrose, and Rudy Vallee sang at the Savoy Hotel. Although the purists claimed that most of this new music was not real *jazz*, there was no denying its popularity – especially when the newly-established 'British Broadcasting Company' began to include dance music in its programme of entertainment.

Marius B. Winter had the distinction of being the first bandleader to broadcast from the studio in Savoy Hill, while saxophonist Ben Davis pioneered the 'outside broadcast' from the ballroom of the Carlton Hotel. Ray Noble recalls: 'Although popular music was severely rationed by the BBC in its early years, these outside broadcasts were getting a tremendous amount of attention. And the music publishers were looking for arrangers. Now I'd written some stuff for a small band we'd got together in London: on the strength of which I got a job as a dance music arranger in Lawrence Wright's Publishing House. So I did arrangements for practically every band in town: for Carroll Gibbons at the Savoy, Ray Starita at the Piccadilly, Bert Ambrose at the Embassy Club.'

Ray Noble and his colleagues churned out dance-band orchestrations by the dozen: mostly of 'show tunes' – hit songs from Broadway musicals by Cole Porter, George Gershwin, Rodgers and Hart. Occasionally, some native talent would emerge to compete with the big guns from the States. Lawrence Wright promoted a new discovery – Horatio Nicholls – who, he claimed, 'was the Greatest Songwriter in the World'. Horatio Nicholls turned out to be a pseudonym for Lawrence Wright himself: even so, he managed to produce a stream of hit songs closely modelled on the American imports: 'The Whispering Pines of Nevada', 'Shalimar', 'Omaha', 'Wyoming Lullaby'.

Lawrence Wright – busy man – was also the founder, editor and publisher of the first magazine devoted to popular music – the *Melody Maker*. In 1927, the paper launched a competition to find the best British dance music orchestrator: and Lawrence Wright was pleased as Punch when it was announced that the first prize had come home to roost in his own office, won by Ray Noble.

The Savoy Orpheans broadcasting their evening performance.
The microphone can be seen above the orchestra

In 1928 the BBC decided to form its own resident dance band. Jack Payne was appointed musical director, and Ray Noble became one of the staff arrangers. He was also starting to write songs of his own: and 'By the Fireside', written and composed with Jimmy Campbell and Reg Connelly, was given its first airing in one of the BBC Dance Orchestra's afternoon broadcasts.

The popularity of dance music broadcasts took everyone by surprise. In 1929 there were ten million listeners: and the experimental 'outside broadcast' had become mass entertainment. Across the country, families were invited to eavesdrop on the restaurants of the Hotel Cecil, the Mayfair, and the Savoy. They could hear the chink of cutlery, the stamp of patent-leather shoes, the murmur of well-bred voices. And the common factor which united the hotel patron and the radio listener was the *foxtrot*. When the BBC announcer invited you to 'Roll up the Carpet and Dance', you did it. You couldn't resist. The music was tuneful, the lyrics were optimistic and cheerful. Ray Noble's 'That's What Life is Made of' sums it up:

> *A little happiness, a little sorrow –*
> *May be awaiting you tomorrow –*
> *That's what life is made of anyhow.*

Carroll Gibbons when he was leader of the Savoy Orpheans

A little tearfulness, a little laughter –
And not a care for what comes after;
There's nothing to be afraid of anyhow.

For the world rolls on the same old way
Just as night comes after day;
And none of us can have a say about it.

So make the most of every minute,
And get your sixty seconds in it,
'Cos that's what life is made of anyhow.

In October 1930 Ray Noble got a call from Carroll Gibbons. 'He was then running the Savoy Hotel Band, as well as being Light Music Director at HMV records; and he told me that he was going to have to give up the recording job, and would I like to have it? I said, "I don't think I can do it": He said, "You might as well try it, to see if you can."

And so I did. And that's how I came to be associated with the New Mayfair Dance Orchestra, which of course has nothing to do with the Mayfair Hotel: it was a band that only came together to make records.'

It was a good time to go into the recording business. A major technological breakthrough – electrical recording – had, by 1925, dramatically improved the sound quality of the discs: huge horned loudspeakers disappeared, and gramophones became portable. From America, the trickle of recordings had become a flood – Paul Whiteman, Guy Lombardo, Fletcher Henderson, the Casa Loma Orchestra – all eagerly awaited by British musicians, anxious to bring their own 'book' up to date with the very latest transatlantic sounds.

For his new HMV band Ray Noble borrowed some of the best instrumentalists from the leading bands of the day. It was acceptable practice for studio bandleaders to use name-band musicians, in their time off; and for the musicians themselves recording was the icing on the cake. A regular West End nightclub job paid between £15 and £25 a week: a three-hour session in a studio was worth £3. The real élite of the business, the aristocrats of the dance-band world, were the 'session musicians', who not only recorded with their regular bands, but – on mornings and afternoons off – with other bands as well.

'The New Mayfair Dance Orchestra' brought together trumpet-player Max Goldberg and trombonist Lew Davis, both from Ambrose; saxophonists George Smith and Bob Wise, together with the whole of the string section from Carroll Gibbons's Savoy Hotel Band; drummer Bill Harty – soon to become Ray Noble's close friend and manager – from Roy Fox; Norman Payne (trumpet) from Elizalde; Nat Gonella (trumpet) from Billy Cotton; plus Harry Jacobson (piano), Albert Harris (guitar), Ernie Riffe and Reg Pink (saxophones).

At first Ray Noble tried a number of different singers: Sam Browne and Elsie Carlisle from Ambrose's band, Jack Plant who sang with Roy Fox, Pat O'Malley (Jack Hylton) and Val Rosing (Harry Hall). Then one day Bill Harty turned up for a session bringing with him an unknown singer whom he introduced to Ray Noble as Al Bowlly. Noble recalls that first encounter:

'I think Al hadn't been in London very long, but Bill Harty said that he was pretty good, and we should give him a try. I asked Al if he sang "printed key" and he said, "Yes". I didn't realise at the time that he was so anxious to get work that if I'd said, "Can you climb trees by your tail?" he'd have said "yes" too! Consequently, the first few records he made with me were a third too high, because his voice was not "printed-key" at all – it was quite a bit lower than that.'

(*Overleaf*) The HMV Band: Ray Noble stands behind the cymbals; Al Bowlly is seated in the foreground

Whatever those initial difficulties, Ray Noble was more than happy to book Al as his vocalist. 'I got along well with him. He trusted my judgment. When I found out his real vocal range, I picked songs more carefully for him. I rehearsed routines with him, and when he unconsciously drifted into things that I didn't think were good, I steered him off. I'd say, "Al, you're singing almost three-quarters of a bar behind in this song because you're trying to sell the pathos of it. You can do it, and still keep a little bit more on the beat, and it will sound better."'

Al listened, and learned. From November 1930, when he made his first record with the New Mayfair Orchestra, 'How Could I be Lonely?' until 1937, when they said goodbye in New York and went their separate ways, Ray Noble rarely used another singer. In the fickle world of dance music it was a most remarkable relationship; and it was the best thing that ever happened to Al Bowlly. He'd come a long way. Born in South Africa of a Lebanese mother and Dutch-Boer father, he travelled to London via Mombasa, Calcutta, Kuala Lumpur, Singapore, Berlin and Munich, singing all the way. With pioneer 'hot' bands on the American model, he refined his vocal technique from the early 'shouting' Jolson style, to the softer 'crooning' that the invention of the microphone dictated. And he also learned how to put a song over with devastating effect. In London, he sang for a few months with Fred Elizalde's Orchestra at the Savoy Hotel. After this promising start, he found himself out of work, and reduced to busking for London theatre queues. The job with Ray Noble came in the nick of time, and soon the legend 'with vocal refrain by Al Bowlly' was a regular feature on the labels of HMV dance-band discs.

The singer was now beginning to emerge from the band as a personality. Before the advent of radio, the vocalist had no particular status. He occupied a chair alongside the musicians, from which he would step forward to the microphone to sing the vocal chorus, before returning to his anonymous place – and perhaps a 'prop' guitar – in the ranks. But the radio listeners insisted on identifying the 'man behind the voice', and the singer became a star. Bing Crosby was the model: soon every band had its own 'crooner', complete with transatlantic drawl, and microphone-hugging technique. Occasionally, a voice was raised in protest. *Punch* railed against 'the new disease – croonitis'; and Rudyard Kipling complained, 'One doesn't feel very national when one is being hummed at by an alien'. Ray Noble made his contribution to the debate in the form of a comic song which was recorded by Jack Buchanan:

The singer as personality:
Al Bowlly with guitar

I'll read Casanova a dozen times over and fret.
The ways of a lover I cannot discover as yet.
Though dozens of ladies consign me to Hades –
    and why?
Like the girl in the yashmak who wanted her
    cash back, I'm shy.

I've got to change my style
I've got to learn to smile
And laugh a little while
I think I can.

I'll hear the voice of spring
And then I'll learn to sing
And make them call me Bing –

(Boo be doo be dooby doo doo) –

I think I can!

From 1930 to 1934, Ray Noble made hundreds of records for HMV. Strangely, his band rarely made a public appearance, although their reputation as a studio band put them top of the league. On the record labels a subtle change was taking place. 'The New Mayfair Dance Orchestra' was replaced in 1932 by 'Ray Noble and the New Mayfair Dance Orchestra'; by 1933 it had become simply 'Ray Noble and his Orchestra'.

His songs, too, were selling well as sheet music. At a time when most middle-class families had a piano at home, Ray Noble songs – mostly slow ballads and so relatively easy to play – became family favourites. If you bought the song-copy, you also got a bonus – the verse of the song, which was often cut from the recorded version, to make it fit onto a ten-inch 78. Ray Noble used the verse in the traditional, music-hall way – as a sort of introduction, to set the scene for the song and give the singer his motivation. This is the little known verse, to one of Ray Noble's best-loved choruses:

I don't need your photograph
To keep by my bed;
Your picture is always in my head.
I don't need your portrait dear,
To call you to mind,
For sleep or waking dear, I find

The very thought of you,
And I forget to do,
The little ordinary things that ev'ryone
  ought to do.
I'm living in a kind of daydream,
I'm happy as a king
And foolish tho' it may seem
To me that's ev'rything. . . .

There were no protest songs in the 1930s. Noël Coward's 'Twentieth Century Blues' was a pastiche, not a cry from the heart: and when Al Bowlly sang 'Buddy, Can You Spare a Dime?' he crooned it like a love lyric. The only song about the Jarrow March was written (by Alan Price) fifty years after the event. Ray Noble and his contemporaries wrote happy-go-lucky songs for people at *play*: for a young audience which was just beginning to learn how to enjoy itself – at the movies, at the race-track, and at the Palais. Although unemployment reached its highest level in 1932, when twenty-one per cent of the population were out of work, still George Orwell could write of 'the queer spectacle of modern electrical science showering miracles upon people with empty bellies. Twenty million people are underfed, but literally everyone in England has access to radio. What we have lost in food, we have gained in electricity. Whole sections of the working class, who have been plundered of all they really need, are being compensated in part by cheap luxuries which mitigate the surface of life. It is quite likely that fish and chips, art silk stockings, tinned salmon, cut-price chocolates, the movies, radio, strong tea and the football pools have between them averted revolution.'

It's unlikely that the bandleaders who broadcast weekly to the nation ever saw themselves in quite this light: certainly, very few of them showed sufficient awareness of their new, national audience to warrant making any changes in their repertoire. What they provided was music for dancing, tailored to the needs of the exclusive minority who could afford to patronise the West End hotels and restaurants. The presence of the BBC microphone, and the sign 'Band Now Broadcasting' meant that the musicians would have to play a bit louder – and that was all. The listeners who tuned in at 10.30 were there on sufferance: they remained on the outside, like the students who were allowed into the balcony of the Monseigneur Restaurant to listen to the Lew Stone Band, and watch the Prince of Wales foxtrot.

In May 1933, Ray Noble's Orchestra made a rare public appearance, at a Cambridge May Ball. The music critic of *Granta*, the University magazine, took the opportunity to make a critical comparison between the Ray Noble and Lew Stone bands:

'Lew Stone is the victim of two evil influences. The first is the one which attacks nearly every dance musician in this country, with the glaring exception of Ray Noble; it is an attempt to copy the idiom of construction employed by the leading negro bands. Lew Stone is also an exponent of the dotted quaver, eight-in-a-bar, slow foxtrot rhythm which becomes, in fact, a victim of the fashionable melodic rhythm of the moment. Ray Noble is probably as different from Lew Stone as any arranger in England today. If he errs anywhere it is on the side of over-orchestration, although his recent record of 'What a Perfect Combination' has proved him to be an arranger capable of producing arrangements in the same idiom as Stone, but of a style greatly superior. His arrangements are always well balanced and constructed and, for the most part, simple. Ray Noble's and Lew Stone's records of 'Won't You Stay to Tea?' form a very interesting comparison.'

After the Cambridge engagement, the Ray Noble Orchestra embarked on its first-ever continental tour. British bands were now beginning to penetrate Europe, following the lead of Jack Hylton and Ambrose, who took a band every year to the Sporting Club in Monte Carlo. Ray Noble was invited to form a band to play at a rather less exotic location – the windy North Sea resort of Scheveningen, in Holland. So he got together some of his regular musicians – Nat Gonella, Tiny Winters, Lew Davis, Bill Harty, Al Bowlly: several of whom brought their wives or girl-friends with them on this 'busman's holiday'. Nat Gonella recalls: 'We had four weeks of hard work and jollity – with the result that, when we got back to England, I had to spend the next two weeks in a nursing home, recuperating from the four weeks in Holland! Say no more....'

The band played in the Kurhaus, the monumental Palace of Fun which still dominates the Scheveningen promenade. Every afternoon, from three-thirty to five-thirty, they played on the terrace for tea-dancers. In the evening they moved indoors to the massive ballroom, where they played from nine o'clock till midnight. Apart from a few last-minute arrangements, the band mostly played scaled-down versions of their established record numbers. 'We didn't need a very large book,' says Ray Noble. 'The French and German holidaymakers only wanted to hear the particular tunes they already knew from our records.' The most requested item was a new foxtrot which Ray Noble had written with Jimmy Campbell and Ray Connelly. Just recorded in England, it

Ray Noble and band flying off to Holland in 1933

was soon to take its place in every dance band's programme, as the music for 'chucking-out time': 'Goodnight, Sweetheart'.

The atmosphere in Scheveningen was relaxed, and friendly. A certain amount of fraternisation between musicians and patrons – which was never tolerated in London – flourished in the Kurhaus: the band played with one eye on their music, and the other on the dance-floor, talent-spotting. 'One night we were playing away,' recalls Ray Noble, 'when a particularly beautiful girl made an entrance. She must have been about twenty or twenty-one – part-Javanese, part-Dutch. She just walked into the room quite quietly and the waiter showed her to the table – and the complete band stopped playing. It's the only time I've ever known a band stop, because she really was the most beautiful thing we'd ever seen in our lives. The only thing that kept going was the drummer, Bill Harty, and he wasn't looking at the time, he was bending down trying to reach something. And so we just had a bass drum going for four beats BOM BOM BOM BOM. And then the band said "Oh God", and picked it up again. It was an extraordinary moment.'

Ray Noble returned from Holland to find some very exciting news awaiting him: he'd had an offer from America. A good many of his recordings were being published there under an arrangement between

HMV and RCA for the exchange of record-masters. These recordings were selling well, especially in colleges, and Ray Noble was invited to go to America, taking Al Bowlly with him, to form a new band with American musicians.

A new restaurant was about to open in New York, on the top floor of the brand-new Rockefeller Centre. This was 'The Rainbow Room' – and Ray Noble was offered the job of resident bandleader. At the same time, MCA invited him to become musical director on a weekly radio show, which was to be sponsored by America's favourite hangover cure, Bromo Seltzer.

Among his fellow-musicians, the news of Ray Noble's American offer was greeted with great excitement, and not a little envy. America was still considered to be 'the Golden Light in the West': to get to New York was the ultimate ambition; to play there was the stuff of dreams. So it was headline news that the Americans wanted Ray Noble. However, before he could take his place on the bandstand of the Rainbow Room, there were a number of obstacles to be overcome: the most formidable of these being the American musician's union – the notorious A.F. of M. On 8 September the *Melody Maker* reported: 'Two well-known American bandleaders have lodged strong protests with the American Federation of Musicians against Noble being allowed to enter America, even though, in order to comply with all the temperamental prejudices of the American musicians, Noble and his sponsors, the Rockwell O'Keefe Bureau, had agreed that the band behind him, with the exception of singer Al Bowlly, should be one hundred per cent American. It was feared that to permit Ray Noble to come to America – the first British bandleader to do so – would set a precedent that might result in a veritable flood of British musicians into the States.'

The irony of this statement was not lost on British musicians, who'd seen the 'veritable flood' of American musicians pouring into London ever since the original Dixieland Jazz band first landed in 1919. Jack Hylton – the only British bandleader other than Ray Noble whose recordings had led to American offers – returned from fruitless meetings with the implacable A. F. of M. and 'whimsically told a *Melody Maker* reporter of a dream he'd had on the voyage.' Conducting the first night of a New York engagement, his downbeat had been greeted by a most extraordinary noise from the band. Amazed and terrified, he saw before him – 'not the famous Hyltonians, but, in the sax section, Danny Polo, Howard Jacobs, Abe Aronsohn and Coleman Hawkins; Louis Armstrong and Roy Fox on trumpets, Jack Harris on violin, and Carroll

A studio still of Paramount's *The Big Broadcast of 1936*, with Noble and Bowlly in action

Gibbons and Charlie Kunz on two pianos.' All, of course, American musicians, welcome and working in London.

On 14 September 1934, with his future still in doubt, Ray Noble sailed on the White Star liner *Majestic*. He deliberately avoided the newspapermen who came to see him off at Waterloo Station: his luggage was put on the boat train but Noble never took his reserved seat.

In New York, the A.F. of M. held its ground. They conceded that Ray Noble would be allowed to coach, and write arrangements for the Rainbow Room Orchestra, which would be led by an American bandleader: it was even suggested that he should go to Toronto, form a band of Canadian musicians, and broadcast to the US from there. Instead, he headed for Hollywood, where he managed to secure for himself a job at

Paramount Studios, writing songs and arrangements for *The Big Broadcast of 1936*. This was a follow-up to the highly successful *Big Broadcast of 1932*, which had launched Bing Crosby on his spectacular career. Bing was also featured in the 1936 edition, and he was thus able to meet for the first time the lanky Englishman whose elegant songs were now part of his own repertoire. A new Ray Noble song was also given its first performance in the film: 'Why Stars Come Out at Night'.

In October, news came from New York that the A. F. of M. had finally relented, and agreed that Noble could take up his job in the Rainbow Room. He still had some weeks to go on his Paramount contract, so an American trombonist and arranger was deputed to organise the band and supervise the first rehearsals. His name was Glenn Miller. George Simon, in his biography of Glenn Miller, wrote: 'And what a band Glenn organised! Charlie Spivak and Pee Wee Irwin played trumpets, Glenn, Tommy Dorsey and Wilbur Schwitzenberg, who later changed his name to Will Bradley, were on trombones; the reeds featured Bud Freeman and Johnny Mince, who later was to star as clarinettist in Tommy Dorsey's band; and the rhythm section consisted of Claude Thornhill on piano, the brilliant George van Eps on guitar, Delmar Kaplan on bass, and Noble's manager, Bill Harty, a not very swinging drummer, who had arrived with Ray from England.'

This came as a surprise to Bill Harty, who'd come to America to act as Ray Noble's 'fixer' – a role in which, some critics said, he seemed more at home than behind the drumkit. He'd certainly never expected to find himself accompanying such a distinguished array of musicians, in the rarefied atmosphere of the Rainbow Room – 'sixty-five stories nearer the stars', as the radio announcers described it. Ray Noble returned from the West Coast in time to his place in front of the band for opening night. He is reputed to have been paid £450 a week, and the boys in the band were earning good money too. They'd even been paid for rehearsals, which was previously unheard of. The band played from Monday to Saturday, from nine o'clock until three a.m. George Simon writes: 'Everything pointed to this becoming one of the great all-round bands of all time. And, for a while, it proved to be just that. Noble, suave and sophisticated, arranged ballads with great musical taste and tenderness. But his English band's jazz efforts had often bordered on the comical. Now, with the jazz-wise Miller taking over that department, the band appeared to have all bases well covered.'

Ray Noble played the part of the elegant English bandleader to perfection – with a little help from violinist Nick Pisani: 'He'd been in

The opening night at the Rainbow Room: Ray
Noble is seated at the piano, and Al Bowlly
is just in the picture at the extreme left

New York a long time and he had a great memory. So that if ever I didn't know who I was talking to, he would whisper in my ear, "He's a very important man, but the girl he's with is not his wife! So don't make the mistake of calling her Mrs So-and-so." Those things are very necessary in our business!' In the early hours of the morning, the dinner-dancers would depart, and the young jazz enthusiasts from the local colleges – from West Point, Harvard, Yale, Annapolis – would arrive: then the band would show off its jazz soloists, until it was time for Al Bowlly to wind up the proceedings, as always, with 'Goodnight Sweetheart'.

And it was in Ray Noble's American band that a now-famous in-strumental sound was born. When trumpeter Pee Wee Irwin – a high-note specialist – left the band, it was discovered that his successor couldn't hit the high notes. In desperation, the top B-flat trumpet part was given to the clarinet, with tenor saxophone doubling an octave lower. In later years, this clarinet-lead combination became known as 'the Glenn Miller sound'.

A year's residence in the Rainbow Room, with weekly broadcasts coast-to-coast, established the Ray Noble Orchestra in the big league of American dance-bands, alongside Lawrence Welk, Carmen Cavallaro, Hal Kemp and Art Kassel. A nationwide tour was organised: 'We went up to Vermont, almost to the Canadian border', Ray Noble recalls. 'Then we went south, right down to Texas. We played one-night stands, college dances, movie theatres where we would do up to five shows a day. At the Paramount in New York we played seven shows a day at the weekend – and that's like living in the dark!'

This American tour provided the inspiration for yet another Ray Noble bestseller. His Victorian predecessor, Leslie Stuart, had found his 'Lily of Laguna' in the wilds of Mississippi: now Ray Noble looked to the West, and discovered his 'child of the prairie' – 'Cherokee':

> Sweet Indian maiden,
> Since first I met you,
> I can't forget you, Cherokee sweetheart.
> Child of the Prairie,
> Your love keeps calling,
> My heart enthralling,
> Cherokee.
>
> Dreams of summertime
> Of lover time gone by
> Throng my memory so tenderly and sigh;

The Band on tour, Catalina Island, California

> *My sweet Indian maiden,*
> *One day I'll hold you*
> *In my arms fold you,*
> *Cherokee.*

After the tour, the band split up. Glenn Miller and Tommy Dorsey went back to New York, to form their own bands; Ray Noble went to Hollywood. On his previous visit, he had come to know George Burns and Gracie Allen, who had taken part in the *Big Broadcast* film. Now they invited him to become musical director on the Burns and Allen

Ray Noble on his return to London in 1938

radio show, and to play a part himself, as an English 'silly-ass' character, in the style of P. G. Wodehouse.

When he returned to England, in April 1938, the self-effacing bandleader was greeted, for the first time, as a celebrity. In the words of
Melody Maker, 'Lionised, feted, and given a rousing reception at Pad-
dington Station, Ray Noble returned to London on Tuesday, to prepare
for his eleven-week tour of key centres throughout the British Isles. He
plans to amplify his American band with a few star English players: in
addition, he is bringing over an American personality girl vocalist,
Mary Manners who, he says, is something out of the ordinary.'

After four years out of the country, Ray Noble encountered a very
different atmosphere in Britain in the years immediately pre-war, and
new trends in popular music. The dance bands had lost some of their
glamour. Musicians were now more likely to find themselves on the
road, doing one-night stands in theatres, town-halls and palais, rather

than enjoying the cosy, dinner-jacketed luxury of the posh clubs and hotels. The elegant, polished music of the early thirties was giving way to something far more boisterous. The biggest hit of 1938 was 'The Lambeth Walk' written by Noël Gay for the musical *Me and my Girl*. It also became a dance craze in the palais: a rolling cockney swagger, with over-the-shoulder thumbing and shouts of 'oi'. Soon everyone was doing it. This was followed, in 1939, by 'Hands, Knees and Boomps-a-Daisy'.

Ray Noble saw the writing on the wall, and went back to Hollywood. His band-leading days were over and, strangely, he never wrote another hit song. He didn't need to: the elegant ballads he had written between 1931 and 1936 provided him with a substantial income for the rest of his days, which he spent in inconspicuous retirement, at first in New Jersey, and subsequently in Santa Barbara, California. His death in a London hospital, in April 1978, came as a shock to dance-music devotees, most of whom didn't know that he had outlived so many of his band-leading contemporaries. His obituarists gave him credit for injecting a truly English note into the Afro-American hybrid that dominated the airwaves throughout the 1930s, and acknowledged him his rightful place in the 'evergreen' section of the popular-music catalogue: a 'musician's composer', and a favourite with singers. The roll-call of artists who have recorded his 'bread and butter' song 'Goodnight Sweetheart' reads like pop music's hall of fame for the last fifty years, and includes every crooner worthy of the name, from Bowlly to Bygraves.

IVOR NOVELLO

'We'll Gather Lilacs'

Ivor Novello rarely patronised the Palais de Danse. He said: 'I want glamour with a capital G. I want great crystal chandeliers, and satin trains fourteen foot long, and footmen in velvet liveries. I want grace, dignity, curtsies and royal salutes.'

And he got what he wanted, in the spectacular musical shows which he created for Drury Lane Theatre between 1935 and 1939. This was theatrical fantasy on the grand scale – so the songs had to be big to match. The situations were dramatic – so every song had to have its moment of drama – a catch in the melody, a hesitation, a moment of poignancy. The style was operatic, calling for trained singers: sopranos, altos, tenors and basses. No crooners, no microphone voices. This was the real thing.

> *I can give you the starlight*
> *Love unchanging and true:*
> *I can give you the ocean,*
> *Deep and tender devotion.*
> *I can give you the mountains,*
> *Pools of shimmering blue,*
> *Call and I shall be*
> *All you ask of me –*
> *Music in Spring*
> *Flowers for a King*
> *All these I bring to you.*

Ivor Novello was born in Cardiff, in 1893. His father was a rent-collector. His mother, Madame Clara Novello Davies, was a large and energetic singing teacher, who had the distinction of becoming the first lady conductor in Wales. Young Ivor was a promising boy soprano and he was sent to Magdalen College Choir School, until his voice broke. He studied harmony and counterpoint with the organist of Gloucester Cathedral, Dr Herbert Brewer, who later declared that Ivor was the laziest pupil he'd ever had.

The family moved to London, and Madame Clara opened a studio in Maida Vale. Ivor spent all his pocket money on visits to the theatre, where he fell under the spell of Gertie Millar, and Lily Elsie – the twin stars of musical comedy. Gertie Millar was the English Rose, in Lionel Monckton's delicate musicals – and Lily Elsie her Viennese rival as Franz Léhar's Merry Widow.

Ivor Novello saw *The Merry Widow* twenty-seven times. He even allowed himself to be dressed up and photographed as a musical comedy beauty. His mother disapproved of all this: and when she found out that he had auditioned for a place in the chorus at Daly's Theatre, she put her foot down. Instead, Ivor became her accompanist for concerts and singing classes. However, she *did* encourage him in his songwriting, and when he was seventeen, a song of his called 'Spring of the Year' was published by the well-known London publisher, Arthur Boosey. It was performed at the Albert Hall by Miss Evangeline Florence accompanied at the piano by the sixteen-year-old composer, in an Eton collar. The song was not well received.

When war broke out, 'Mam' suggested that he should try his hand at writing a patriotic song. He was disinclined, but then she set about writing one herself which was so awful that, in order to prevent her trying to publish it, Ivor sat down and wrote a suitably stirring tune. A friend, Lena Guilbert Ford, suggested some lyrics, which Ivor wasn't satisfied with. Off the top of his head, he then produced the opening line 'Keep the Home Fires Burning', which was added to Miss Ford's 'Till the boys come home', to make the song that soon became the anthem of the Home Front. When it was first performed, by Sybil Vane, at the Alhambra Theatre, the young composer was astonished to hear the audience begin to join in on the second chorus, although they'd never heard the song before. The Grenadier Guards' band, which was taking part in the concert, also began to play an impromptu accompaniment: in all, the song was repeated eight times, with ever-increasing enthusiasm.

Ivor went to France with a concert-party, to introduce his new song to the troops in person. Soon 'Keep the Home Fires Burning' was being used as a catchphrase in advertisements and propaganda posters. The

Ivor Novello at Magdalen College Choir School, 1903

song earned him £15,000 in royalties over the next four years. It also made him a celebrity. A young poet, Robert Graves, paid him a visit at his flat in the Aldwych, opposite the Gaiety Theatre: 'I found him in an atmosphere of incense and cocktails. He and his young stage friends were all sitting or lying on cushions scattered about the floor. Feeling uncomfortably military, I removed my spurs (I was a temporary Field

(*Overleaf*) Ivor Novello with Carol Dempster
in a still from the D. W. Griffith film, *The White Rose*

Officer at the time) in case anyone got pricked. Novello had joined the Royal Naval Air Service, but, his genius being officially recognised, was allowed to Keep the Home Fires Burning, until the boys came home.'

In fact, Flight Sub-Lieutenant Novello, I., had been grounded after a disastrous first training flight. The playwright, Ben Travers, who was his instructor, claims, 'If it hadn't been for me, Ivor wouldn't have survived the war!' He was posted to Chingford, where he caused another fuss by wearing a uniform made by his own tailor of non-regulation material, with non-regulation badges. At the same time, he refused to allow the RNAS to interfere with his social and theatrical life: in 1916, he contributed songs to a number of West End shows – *The Bing Boys are Here* (starring George Robey), *Theodore & Company* (in which he collaborated with Jerome Kern), and *See-Saw* (produced by André Charlot). He also wrote a song for Jack Buchanan: 'And her Mother Came Too'.

After the war, Ivor went to America – and his mother came too. They spent five months in New York, during which time Ivor saw as many plays as he could cram in. He resolved to become an actor. The following year, as if in answer to his prayers, he was offered a leading role in a silent movie drama *The Call of the Blood*. The director, Louis Mercantor, gave Ivor the part without ever having seen him in the flesh, and despite his total lack of acting experience or training. A photograph of his fine profile was enough to win him the part.

That same noble profile caught the eye of American director, D. W. Griffith, across the dining room of the Savoy Hotel. Six months later Ivor found himself in New York, filming *The White Rose* opposite Mae Marsh, and acclaimed as 'the new Valentino'. He started writing his own screenplays, and, coupling himself with Constance Collier under the pseudonym 'David L'Estrange', wrote a melodrama about a Parisian bounder, *The Rat*. It was first produced as a stage play, in 1924. *London Opinion* commented: 'As a work of art the value of *The Rat* is about ninepence at a liberal estimate, but as a box-office attraction, I should think it ranks about £1,500 a week.' The following year, it was made into a film which was so successful that it became a series: *The Triumph of the Rat* and *The Return of the Rat* followed in subsequent years.

From 1920 to 1930, Ivor Novello combined three careers – actor, playwright and composer – with equal measure of success. He starred in twenty-one silent films. He appeared in nineteen plays in London and New York – ten of which he had written himself. He composed the music for fifteen musical plays and revues. And he joined Noël Coward in the

Noël Coward visiting the set during filming of
his play *The Vortex*, in which Ivor Novello starred

full glare of the showbiz publicity spotlight – invited to every party, expected at every first night. They also shared one of the most spectacular theatrical flops of the decade, when Ivor starred in Noël's *Sirocco*,
which was booed by the audience and blasted by the press. Even so, they
remained close friends. Looking back on their relationship, Noël
Coward wrote: 'We have much in common. We were both boy-sopranos
and we both drink a lot of tea. We both work hard and are fortunate,
talented and successful. We are both reviled by the Press, and respected
by the public.'

The identification was taken even further in a revue sketch by Herbert Farjeon, in which a forgetful actress, dictating her memoirs, says:
'If it wasn't Noël, it was usually Ivor. I hardly knew which was which!'

José Collins, star of *The Maid of the Mountains*, remembered the pair more vividly. In her autobiography, she recalls: 'Ivor's flat was just across the road from the Gaiety, and he and Noël used to arrive at my flat in time for lunch or tea. After lunch we used to switch on my big wireless and spend hours, we three, tuning in to stations all over Europe and the USA. When "Uncle Caractacus" sang in the Children's Hour on the wireless, Ivor and Noël used to go to the piano and do an impersonation. Noël sang while Ivor played. They are both mimics and both screamingly funny.'

In 1931, Ivor went to Hollywood. MGM had bought the screen rights to his play *The Truth Game*, and he was put under contract to prepare a screenplay. However, he soon discovered that the producers wanted to change almost everything in the play except the names of the characters and the title. Besides, he was homesick and when news came of the death of his father, he was allowed to break his contract and return home. Although *The Truth Game* was never filmed, Ivor's name did appear on the credits of another MGM film – *Tarzan and the Ape Man*, for which he wrote the dialogue.

He decided to give up the movies, and concentrate on the theatre. In the summer of 1934, he was invited to lunch by the London impresario, H. M. Tennant, at the Ivy Restaurant. They talked of the financial troubles of Drury Lane Theatre, which was going through a bad patch. Up until 1930, this huge theatre had been kept solvent by a number of successful American musical shows – *Rose Marie, The Desert Song, Showboat*; but, since Noël Coward's *Cavalcade* in 1930, it had played host to a series of disastrous flops. On the spur of the moment Ivor said to Tennant, 'Why don't you ask me to write a show for Drury Lane?' There and then he produced a preposterous story, of a Ruritanian monarch and his gypsy mistress (who happens also to be an opera singer) who become involved with a young Englishman (who happens to have invented a new system of television). Among other spectacular events, it included a Romany wedding, a revolution and a shipwreck. Almost unchanged, this became the plot of *Glamorous Night*, which opened at Drury Lane on 2 May 1935.

Although he was no singer, Ivor Novello gave himself a leading role in *Glamorous Night* – as the non-singing inventor Anthony Allan. He wanted to be on stage on the opening night. He said: 'In a busy and not unexciting life, I have had many thrills and many adventures. But no thrill I have ever known and no adventure I have ever undertaken has given me the tremendous thrill which Drury Lane has provided. For I,

The gypsy wedding
in *Glamorous Night*

like every member of my profession, have the greatest veneration and respect for this grand theatre, which is more national than any specially founded "National Theatre" could ever be.

'Up to this year it had never been my luck to appear there. The nearest I ever got to it was when I played the piano "offstage" at a charity matinee. But I believe that everything comes to him who waits – more especially if he helps it along! – and I hoped that one day I would have a chance. That chance came. Drury Lane wanted a show. I made up my mind that the show would be mine. And here I am!'

Glamorous Night set the style for the shows that followed: part operetta, part musical comedy, part melodrama. Soon audiences came to know what to expect from 'a Novello show' – and they remained loyal for the next fifteen years. The Royal Family came to see *Glamorous Night*:

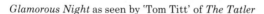

Glamorous Night as seen by 'Tom Titt' of *The Tatler*

the Queen was in tears by the final curtain. The Theatre critics were more objective, though not unfriendly. The *Telegraph* said: 'If it is nonsense, it is glamorous nonsense, and for those who are ready to be entertained, it is the best show of its kind Drury Lane has had for years.' *The Observer* went further: 'I lift my hat to Mr Novello. He can wade through tosh with the straightest face: the tongue never visibly approaches the cheek.'

Mary Ellis, who sang the soprano lead, confirms that there was never any question of the cast 'sending up' the material – however unlikely the situations in which they found themselves. She recalls: 'I used to spend my wits and my spirit on a scene which, if it had been done less well, would have been ghastly. If it had been done badly or cheaply, it would never have worked.'

Besides, it was the *music* that mattered. The story was a decorative framework around the string of glorious melodies that soon became equally popular outside the theatre: 'Glamorous Night', 'Shine Through my Dreams', 'Waltz of June', 'When the Gypsy Played', 'Fold Your Wings' – to this day, Ivor's songs never fail to strike a chord with the incurably romantic.

Glamorous Night played to capacity audiences until the end of the year, when H. M. Tennant took it off to make room for the traditional Christmas pantomimes. This was a disastrous mistake: the theatre started losing money again, and Novello was commissioned to write another musical as quickly as possible. *Careless Rapture* was the result, with an even more preposterous plot, in which the bastard son of a duke pursues a musical comedy actress from Hampstead Heath to China, surviving an earthquake en route. As before, Novello himself played the romantic lead – and he even found a way of allowing himself to sing a few bars.

MICHAEL (appearing at the studio window) Can I have a singing lesson?
MADAME Oh ... and have you a voice?
MICHAEL I shouldn't think so ... I've never tried.
MADAME Then try now.
MICHAEL (sings) Ahh!
          (speaks) Who did that?
MADAME You did.
MICHAEL Did I? You know, I think I'd be better in opera!
PENNY I think you'd be better in Gaol.
MICHAEL No, opera ... the food's better. (He sings)

105

Careless Rapture: dream-sequence in the Chinese temple

The American actress Dorothy Dickson played the part of Penny in *Careless Rapture*. A week before it opened, she got a telephone call from Ivor: 'He said to me "Can you come down to the theatre tomorrow morning at ten o'clock: they're delivering the earthquake!" So we all went down, and there it was – all collapsed! Ivor said, "Isn't it Heaven?" and we all passed out laughing. But there was another side to Ivor: he could be very down-to-earth, even ruthless at times.'

Even before *Careless Rapture* finished its six months' run at Drury

Careless Rapture: an impression of the production by 'Tom Titt' in *The Tatler*

Lane Novello was already preparing his next musical. He worked at tremendous speed, and the songs poured out of him. 'If a thing does not come at once, quite spontaneously, I scrap it immediately and wait for another idea to come along. And I never waste time on the details – on things the audience won't even notice. No, I've got to get right at their hearts – right at their solar plexus.'

He composed at the piano, breaking one of the cardinal rules of composition. Doctor Herbert Brewer would have strongly disapproved. But Ivor was an inveterate improviser: he spent hours sitting at the piano, allowing his fingers to stray over the keys until the particular shape of a melody, or combination of harmonies, appealed to him sufficiently to warrant him writing it down or, in later years, recording it on his tape machine. The tune invariably came first, then he would add the words himself, or give them to Christopher Hassall, who was his lyricist from *Glamorous Night* onwards. Once the song was complete, Ivor would hand it over to a professional orchestrator. He showed no interest in the detail of the orchestral scoring or the instrumentation. He said: 'Whatever strange harmonies you invent, the integral thing is the melody. You reach a greater number of people through melody than through any other quality. It is the *melody* that lasts in peoples' minds – years after the harmonies and complicated arrangements are forgotten.'

He had a penchant for those particular chords – musicians call them 'flattened thirteenths' – which suggest a stirring of the emotions, especially when drawn out in a poignant rallentando. His own favourite composers were Debussy, Ravel, Delius and Puccini. He once admitted to liking 'nothing earlier than Wagner'. But his greatest love was Elgar, whose oratorios he used to sing in the choir at Magdalen College, an early love which lasted. He was once asked to which school of British composers he thought he belonged. He replied: 'Viewed dispassionately, I am sort of betwixt and between: if there was a hymn that was neither ancient nor modern, it would be me.'

Coronation Year, 1937, was just the time for a new patriotic song, to open the new Novello show at Drury Lane, *Crest of the Wave*. It was sung as the curtain went up, by forty knights in Crusader armour, and reprised, later in the play, by a Pageant of Ghosts:

> *Rose of England,*
> *Though shalt not fade here.*
> *Proud and bright*
> *From rolling year to year.*

The knights in Crusader costume at the opening of *Crest of the Wave*

Red shall thy petals be
As rich as wine untold,
Shed by thy warriors,
Who served thee of old.

Rose of England,
Breathing England's air,
Flower of liberty beyond compare:
With hand and heart endure
To cherish thy prime
Though shalt blossom to the end of time.

Other songwriters used very different methods to tap the patriotic fervour that gripped the country in the pre-war years. People seemed to want to get together and *sing*; so noisy 'sing-along' songs like 'The Lambeth Walk', 'Run, Rabbit, Run', and 'Knees up, Mother Brown' became increasingly popular – in pubs, in palais, at football grounds, and on the radio.

Ivor Novello refused to allow any of this to touch him. He bought a beautiful house in the country – 'Redroofs', near Maidenhead – where he held court, surrounded by glamorous people. Christopher Hassall observed that Ivor at Redroofs 'always gave the impression of being a distinguished visitor from the Balkans ... although beautiful and artistic, the house always seemed to be the refuge of an exiled heir to a kingdom who has made his home in England'.

In March 1939, *The Dancing Years* opened at Drury Lane. Although set, again, in Old Vienna, its theme was not entirely removed from the world outside the theatre. During rehearsals, Ivor wrote a speech which he would deliver himself as the persecuted composer Rudi Kleber. It's the nearest he ever came to making a political statement.

'We shall see great changes and feel it here – times of unrest and anger and hatred in the world – and these things are strong. We shall almost forget to laugh and make music, but we shan't quite forget, and some day we'll wake up, as from an evil dream and the world will smile again and forget to hate, and the sweetness of music and friendliness will once more be important. . . .'

The war closed Drury Lane, but *The Dancing Years* survived. It was produced on tour by Tom Arnold, for eighteen months: and then re-installed in London at the Adelphi Theatre. It was still playing in 1943 when Madame Clara Novello Davies died. It was a terrible blow to Ivor, who worshipped her, despite the many eccentricities that she'd begun to display in later years, when her enthusiasm for a pet project carried her to a point far beyond her means. All too often, Ivor would receive a panic-stricken telegram from New York, Toronto, or Caracas: 'AM YOUR MOTHER'S LAWYER SHE IS IN DIRE FINANCIAL DIFFICULTIES CREDITORS PRESSING HER COURT PROCEEDINGS INSTITUTED LANDLORD EVICTING HER FROM FLAT YOU MUST CABLE FIVE HUNDRED POUNDS IMMEDIATELY TO AVOID EMBARRASSING PUBLICITIES FOR FURTHER DETAILS CABLE ME FANHOLTLAW HOLTZMANN.'

Mam shared in all her son's great triumphs: she attended every first night, an imposing figure in the stage box, dressed always in white with her silver hair piled high. At the curtain call, Ivor's first bow was inevitably to her. She died with only one ambition unrealised – a plan to fly her Welsh Ladies' Choir to Berlin and sing Hitler into surrender.

For Ivor, other trials lay ahead. The following year, he was summonsed for a breach of the wartime petrol restrictions when it was discovered that he had been using his Rolls Royce to drive from the theatre to Redroofs. He appeared at Bow Street, and was sentenced

Ivor Novello as the persecuted
Rudi Kleber in *The Dancing Years*

to two months in prison. On appeal, this was reduced to one month: and, in a blaze of hostile publicity, Ivor Novello was sent to Wormwood Scrubs.

The prison chaplain, the Rev. Meredith Davies, went out of his way to alleviate Ivor's ordeal. At first he was given the task of helping to build a new stage for the prison theatre: but when it became clear that he was totally unsuited to hard labour, the chaplain arranged for him to be transferred to the prison library. There he was set to work repairing torn books, but even this proved too difficult, so finally, he was put to making scrap books for illiterate prisoners. He was locked in his cell from 4.30 p.m. till 6.30 a.m. on weekdays, and at weekends from 4.30 p.m. on Saturday until 6.30 a.m. on Monday. He described his feelings, in a document written after the first two weeks' imprisonment: 'When I talk to people with long sentences – five years, eighteen months – mine seems a fleabite, but the relative quality doesn't impress me at all. I just hate, loathe and despise every second of it and I pray God to let me forget it all as soon as possible. Of course, I shan't be able to avoid talking about it at first and my friends will be curious, but I shall never be betrayed into rushing into print. In fact, officially, I shall say nothing.

'One thing has disappointed me. I have always been surrounded by people – never alone; I had an idea that if I was alone I should "find myself" – discover some rare new philosophy, some staggering new revelation – find a new depth of soul – but no, not at all. I have learned nothing. I'm just the same – only very angry and resentful. Perhaps it is possible that, when I get home, my having suffered a lot and having been so terribly lonely *will* do something for me but I very much doubt it. . . .

'Oh, Christ Jesus help me to get through this and come out *sane* – I think the root of insanity is sheer, utter, futile, black boredom.'

He told the Rev. Davies that he would not return to the theatre after his release: however, he was persuaded by his friends that public opinion *would* support him, and indeed there was a growing feeling that justice had overdone it, and used his case as a means to publicise the penalties of black-market dealing.

On 20 June 1944 Ivor walked from his flat in the Aldwych to the Adelphi Theatre. At the stage door, he posed for photographers, and gave an interview to 'Peter' of the *Daily Mail*. Just as the curtain went up, the sirens sounded for a flying bomb raid. When Ivor made his first entrance, through a crowd of waltzing figures, the audience exploded. W. Macqueen-Pope, who was in the audience, described the moment:

Ivor Novello in *Lederhosen* for *The Dancing Years*
poses with his mother. Before the run ended, she was dead

'A hurricane of applause, a vast wave of enthusiasm, swept across the huge theatre. It came from all parts, it grew in volume, not merely hand-clapping, but shouts and cheers – a warmth of friendly feeling, long pent up, but now finding a public outlet. It was the verdict of the public who knew the man. What Ivor's own sensations were must be his own secret. But the thunder of welcome seemed to take him by surprise. He stood facing the audience, stooping a little, looking his usual charming self, but very strangely young and a little helpless. His smile flashed, there was a trace of nervousness in it, and in his hanging arms. And who could wonder? For it was an ordeal in itself to stand up to such applause at any time – and at a moment so fraught with emotion, a harder task still, however gratifying. But the applause lasted for over two minutes – an unprecedented time – and he recovered quickly. His smile got its genuine beam, he bowed his usual boyish bow – and then he turned and started the scene ... he was Ivor Novello again ... And as if in complete sympathy, the "All Clear" sounded outside the theatre.'

He received thousands of letters – all of which he kept, in his study at

Redroofs. Thereafter he rarely spoke of his experience, although his friend Heather Thatcher recalls an occasion when 'we were driving down to Redroofs, and I said "Ivor, the Rolls looks marvellous. Is it a new one?" And he said, "No, I've just had the arrows painted out."'

Within weeks of his release from prison, Ivor was in France, entertaining the troops in an ENSA company which also included Margaret Rutherford. They performed a play based on an Agatha Christie story – 'Love from a Stranger'. After the play, a piano was wheeled on to the stage, and the company would lead the troops in a sing-song. Ivor used these occasions to try out a new song he'd just written, which he hoped might one day rival the popularity of his First World War hit – 'Keep the Home Fires Burning'. In due course, with a little help from Vera Lynn, it did just that. It was 'We'll Gather Lilacs'.

The song duly took its place in the next Novello musical, *Perchance to Dream*. This was the first show for which Novello wrote both words and music; since Christopher Hassall – who'd been his lyric-writer since 1935 – was in the army. Otherwise, it was the formula as before. James Agate said: 'The curtain, when it went up, took with it the entire audience which remained in seventh heaven until, after three hours and a half, the curtain descended and automatically brought the audience down with it.'

In the last act, Ivor – in the role of Sir Graham Rodney, Regency Buck and ex-highwayman – is discovered sitting in the twilight at the piano. The action of the scene required him to play a few chords as a cue for the entrance of a footman. One night, to the astonishment of the orchestra, the cast and, indeed, of Ivor himself, he found himself playing a new waltz tune, which had occurred to him at that very moment. Muttering to himself 'This is good ... this is good,' he whispered to the actor playing the footman to go and fetch him a pencil and paper, so that he might write it down before he forgot it. This same little tune was to become one of his biggest hits: 'Some Day my Heart Will Awake'.

For the next four years, there were no new Novello shows. He was ill, and went to Jamaica to convalesce. Meanwhile, a new American invasion was under way: musicals by Rodgers and Hart, Oscar Hammerstein and Irving Berlin were establishing a bridgehead in the West End, and capturing audiences by the thousand. In 1949 Ivor responded to this challenge by staging a retreat to 'Murania – Land of Song and Liberty', where the king's in exile and the peasants are revolting. This was to be the last of the Novello spectaculars. It was called *King's Rhapsody*. As always, the romantic lead was played by the author: but

The case of *King's Rhapsody* seen with the
caricaturist's eye of 'Tom Titt'

this time he had to create for himself the part of an older man (he was
now 56) in Crown Prince Nikki, who returns to his native Murania to
become king after twenty years in exile, seduces his intended bride (a
Scandinavian princess masquerading as a maid), supports a peasant
uprising, and abdicates in favour of the son of this pre-emptive union.
He returns incognito for the coronation of the boy-king. Afterwards,
alone in the empty cathedral, he picks up a white rose which the Snow
Princess has left for him on the steps of the altar. Slow curtain. . . . The
orchestra plays the final reprise of 'The Gates of Paradise': not a dry eye
in the house.

The critical response to *King's Rhapsody* was lukewarm. The *Daily
Mail* said: 'It is very much the mixture as before: just the desired blend of
champagne and sugar.' The drama critic of *Punch* described it as: 'A
vast insipid musical in which Ivor Novello has pulled out most of the
stops in the organ of easy sentiment.'

Ivor had an answer to those who berated him for being popular: 'I give
the public what I would like to see myself. We of the theatre write and
act to please the public, to "fill the plush", to convey our emotions
across the footlights and share our rhapsodies with the audience.
No matter how good a play or an operetta may seem to be, if it fails to
draw an audience, then to my mind it ceases to exist, to have any useful
purpose.'

King's Rhapsody was Ivor's greatest commercial success. He used to

115

cause his manager, Tom Arnold, some embarrassment by writing the nightly takings in greasepaint on his dressing-room mirror. And to this day, a number of theatre charities, to whom he bequeathed all his future royalties, enjoy a substantial income from new productions that are staged – year in, year out – all over the world.

After *King's Rhapsody*, Ivor was asked what he was planning to do next. He said: 'I don't know. But I really can't go on doing this Ruritania business very much longer.'

His parting shot was *Gay's the Word*. With tongue firmly in cheek he wrote a lively contemporary musical about a middle-aged trouper who finds herself being driven out of the business by the new generation. Alan Melville wrote the lyrics – although it did take him some time to adapt to Novello's disconcerting method of composition:

'He would put his specs on, run his fingers up and down the keyboard, and then go into a melody that in nine cases out of ten was very nearly the finished article! Apart from bursting at the seams with tunes, he seemed to sense exactly where the stresses were. There was only one snag about him as a collaborator: he adored sneezing – he was absolutely kinky about it. And once Mr Novello started sneezing he was a very difficult man to stop. "It flushes out the system," he said; and the poor old lyricist had to stand by until the LP was over.'

The show was directed by Jack Hulbert and the 'Gay' of the title was played, with amazing energy, by Cicely Courtneidge. When the curtain goes up, her last show – a sadly old-fashioned musical comedy – is dying on its feet in Manchester:

> *Ruritania!*
> *The former delights*
> *Of Glamorous Nights*
> *No longer constitutes a raving mania*
> *In Ruritania.*
> *Ruritania!*
> *Rhapsodical Kings*
> *No longer are things*
> *To sing about in Greece or in Albania*
> *Or Ruritania!*
> *Our nights are now*
> *No longer considered glamorous:*
> *Since Oklahoma*
> *We've been in a coma*
> *And no one cares for us.*

Ruritania!
As nobody cares
For foreign affairs
We're going swiftly down the drain-i-ain-i-er
In Ruritania!
Ruritania!
In spite of all those
American shows
You'll see us all back again at Drury Laneia
From Ruritania!

The show (within a show) is, predictably, a flop: and Gay decides to open a drama school in Folkestone. But she finds her first crop of students sadly lacking in ability, and gives them a lecture on the qualities that are needed to get to the top:

Vitality
The stars who gain'd their immortality
Knew with finality the practicality
Of something that's lacking in us.
They all had vitality plus!

D'you remember Gertie Millar, no you wouldn't
I'm afraid
Seymour Hicks and Vesta Tilley's swagger cane?
Lily Elsie as the 'Widow'
Jose Collins as the 'Maid'
Dear old Robey, Billy Merson at the Lane –
Some gone, and some who still, are the tops
of any bill,
Give me Gracie Fields in place of any crooner –
Hetty King still debonair,
Phyllis Dare and Zena Dare
G. H. Elliott in the Lily of Laguna –
Let the charm school keep on charming
Let the Bobby soxers fawn!
If you want to see vitality
See Dorothy and Shaun!
All the stars of the past are remembered today
And the reason they last
They were Gay! Gay! Gay!

There was no part for Ivor himself in *Gay's the Word*: besides, he was

117

'Nikki of Murania' faced with abdication. A late portrait of
Ivor Novello from the souvenir programme of *King's Rhapsody*

still playing Prince Nikki in *King's Rhapsody* when *Gay's the Word* opened at the Saville Theatre on 15 February 1951. He made the opening night, although he was unwell, and, for the first time in sixteen years, failed to take his first night curtain call from the stage.

Next day, the *Evening Standard* proclaimed: 'Once more Ivor Novello proves that he is immortal without being divine. No Richard Rodgers, Cole Porter or Irving Berlin can dethrone him. It is time that some official recognition was shown of his achievement in keeping the British flag flying over Ruritania.'

Sadly, before anyone could take up the suggestion, Ivor Novello died, of a coronary thrombosis. It happened in the early hours of 6 March 1951, in his flat above the Aldwych Theatre in the Strand. Only a few hours earlier, as Prince Nikki of Murania, he'd abdicated in favour of his twelve-year-old son.

> NIKKI He's on his own now. He mustn't faint, he's a King. They'll
>   hold the crown over his head – it's too big and too heavy for
>   him to wear. I found it too big and too heavy and I was a
>   grown man, and he's only a little boy.

Ivor Novello's funeral was like a coronation – the streets were lined with crowds all the way. The funeral service was broadcast 'live' from Golders Green cemetery. For close friends and relatives, a recording was played back that evening in the BBC's Aeolian Hall. It was, almost, a national day of mourning. W. Macqueen-Pope later described the scene at Golders Green:

'A line three-deep of waiting people, stretching further than the eye could see . . . Women predominated . . . There were smart women in fur coats but they were in the minority. Most of his audience were middle-class and working-class people . . .

'The man they mourned had opened the doors of a different life, had given them glimpses of that world they liked to see but could never enter, had cheered them and stirred them with his gift of music and song . . . had given them, for a brief hour or so, the thing in which he so deeply and sincerely believed – Romance.'

LIONEL BART

'Fings Ain't Wot They Used T'Be'

In Lionel Bart's family, the children slept three to a bed. Lionel was born the youngest of twelve children, to Maurice and Yelta Begleiter, in the East End of London, on 1 August 1930. His father was an immigrant tailor, who worked seven days a week, twelve hours a day, to support his huge family. 'Since that time', says Lionel, 'I've never allowed myself to think poor. When I became extremely rich, and they told me I was earning £16 a minute, I figured I could spend £8 a minute. Of course, I was wrong: but, with hindsight I *wasn't* wrong because I had a great time doing it.'

He spent his childhood picking up fruit, pickled herrings and rude expressions around the stalls of Petticoat Lane. He discovered that he had a flair for inventing new words for popular songs, thus making them even more popular with his pals. He was the first in the gang to know all the rude words to 'My Old Man's a Dustman', 'Eskimo Nell', and 'Maggie May'. His father bought him a violin, but Lionel never learnt to play it. He wanted to become an artist: and when he was thirteen, in the year of his barmitzvah, he won a scholarship to St Martin's School of Art. He did his National Service in the RAF, where the only plane he saw was a vintage Spitfire embedded in concrete at the station gates. The only mark he left on the Service was a huge mural which he painted on the NAAFI wall.

Demobbed in 1953, he got a job as a scene-painter, at the left-wing Unity Theatre in King's Cross. He recalls: 'Alfie Bass was working there, and he was going to produce a revue. And he put a notice on the board saying, "Does anybody want to write songs for this revue?" It was to be a topical revue about the Coronation, called *Turn it Up*. I saw this

'The Cavemen': Mike Pratt, Tommy Steele and Lionel Bart

notice, and as I'd already written a couple of songs, I gave them to Alfie. A couple of days later, he came down to the scenery-painting bay and said to me, "Come on out of there, son – you're a songwriter." And I guess it's all down to Alfie Bass really: it was he made me realise I could write lyrics and tunes, and put them together.'

Tin Pan Alley in the early 1950s was a property ripe for redevelopment. The dawn of the new Elizabethan Age saw the birth of a new creature – the teenager, whose musical appetites no longer coincided with those of his parents' generation. The music of the dance bands, the songs of Ivor Novello, were already a bit passé; even the penetrating voices of the balladeers – Ann Shelton, David Whitfield, Joan Regan, Donald Peers – failed to reach the ears of the young. The teenager wanted something new, and something he could call his own. It arrived in 1954, courtesy of a middle-aged American bandleader, with an unshakeable quiff of hair glued to his forehead, and a rhythm section that

122

played as squarely on the beat as Victor Sylvester. 'Shake, Rattle and Roll' was the invitation; and soon every teenage party thrilled to the music of Bill Haley and his Comets.

For professional musicians, this was the end of the world. Saxophonists, trumpet-players and violinists were appalled: the spectre of guitar-wielding yobbos ousting twenty-piece dance bands from the palais and clubs was too horrible to contemplate. But it happened. Doomsday had arrived, and Lionel Bart wrote a song in celebration:

> *On the first day there'll be lightning*
> *On the second, there'll be hail*
> *The third daybreak there'll be a big*
> *   earthquake*
> *So brother forward your mail.*
>
> *The fourth day there'll be darkness*
> *The last time the sun has shone*
> *The fifth day you'll wake up and say*
> *   the world's* REAL GONE.
>
> *Rock and Roll you sinners!*
> *Sing to save your soul,*
> *There ain't no room for beginners*
> *When the world starts to rock and roll.*
>
> *Rock and Roll you sinners!*
> *Sing to be alive*
> *There ain't no room for beginners*
> *When the world starts to jive.*

In 1956 Lionel Bart got together with two friends to form a group. In common with most other embryonic rock'n'rollers, they could neither afford, nor play, the amplified instruments that made the right noises. So Bart's band initially was a skiffle group, featuring ex-Merchant Seaman Tommy Hicks (later to become Tommy Steele) on acoustic guitar, Mike Pratt on tea-chest bass, and Lionel Bart (who couldn't read a note of music) on washboard. They called themselves 'The Cavemen', and they played, appropriately enough, in 'The Cave' – a café under the Arches of Waterloo station. Previously an SPO Joint (Sausage, Potato and Onion), it soon acquired the superior status of coffee bar, rivalling Soho establishments like 'The Breadbasket', 'The Nucleus' and 'The Two I's', where other would-be rock'n'roll stars were cutting their teeth on skiffle: Reg Smith (later Marty Wilde), Terry Nelhams (Adam Faith), and Harry Webb (Cliff Richard).

The record companies and music publishers sent their 'A and R' (Artists and Repertoire) men to comb these coffee bars for likely talent. Soon The Cavemen had a record contract, and an advance against royalties which gave them sufficient funds to electrify their instruments. There was no place for a washboard in the new line-up, so Bart retired as a musician and became a full-time songwriter. That same year, a song by Bart, Pratt and Steele – 'Rock with the Caveman' – went to number one in the newly-established Top Twenty, above 'Lay Down Your Arms', 'Nellie the Elephant' and 'Elizabethan Serenade'.

'The Cavemen' became 'The Steelemen', and Tommy Steele became the first British rock'n'roll star. Over the next three years, songs by Bart, Pratt and Steele were invariably hits: 'A Handful of Songs', 'Water, Water', 'Tommy the Toreador', and 'Little White Bull'. Lionel Bart realised the first stage of his considerable ambition, by becoming a wealthy man. The *Daily Mail* printed a photograph of Bart in the bath, under the caption: *Picture a Man Earning £3 in 4 minutes*. Their reporter discovered that: 'Four minutes is the time it takes for an average pop record to play. £3 is Lionel's share of the royalties . . . and there are a lot of hits. While Lionel bathes, he can hear himself making money with any one of a dozen 'top-of-the-pops': if he never did another day's work, he would be able to live in luxury for the rest of his days. You would think that Lionel Bart would be among the happiest of men . . . in fact, he is not. Life for Lionel is one long frustration. Reclining on a chi-chi black sofa, in his fashionable mews flat in Kensington, Mr Bart told me wistfully: "I was much happier when I had my first fifteen shillings in my pocket. Success is tough. Let's face it, if you're an artist you can't just sit back counting your money. It's tough knowing what to do next."'

In the event, he turned back to his first love – the theatre. He met up with Joan Littlewood, whose Theatre Workshop productions at the Theatre Royal, Stratford East, were beginning to make an impact on the local East End community, as well as winning audiences away from her 'up-market' rivals in Shaftesbury Avenue. At Stratford, exuberant, improvised entertainment was the order of the day, and for a new play by Frank Norman about the Soho underworld, entitled *Fings Ain't Wot They Used T'Be*, Lionel Bart was invited to write some songs – in a hurry. He recalls:

'There was no money: all the actors were on about £15 a week – and I'm talking about people like Richard Harris, James Booth, Barbara Windsor, Yootha Joyce. There was no time either: we had just two weeks to put a show on

Joan Littlewood directing *Fings*. In the background,
Lionel Bart leans against the set

– write it, rehearse it, stage it. I was sitting in the stalls writing the songs, while
the actors were improvising their dialogue with Frank Norman: when the songs
came up, I ran on the stage and taught them to the actors. It was an amazing two
weeks. In fact, even on the opening night, when the critics were in, Joan
Littlewood got hold of me in the interval and told me to write a new song, find
myself a costume, and appear myself as a totally new character at three separate
cues, in the second half! Which I did. I found an old trenchcoat down in the
basement and an old bowler hat, blacked a tooth out, got some spoons from the
canteen, borrowed a pair of maracas from the drummer in the pit, and I came on
as 'Meatface'. It was crazy . . . but, looking back, it was the most enjoyable thing
I've done in my life, in terms of the theatre.'

Fings opened in February 1959. The Wolfenden Report and the new
Street Offences Act were then headline news: and the title of the show
was a tart's complaint against the new order.

> *I used to lead a lovely life of sin,*
> *Dough, I charged a ton!*

125

Now it's become an under-cover game.
Who wants to read a postcard in a window
'Massaging done?'
Somehow the Bus'ness doesn't seem the same
It's a very different scene,
Well you know what I mean.

There's toffs wiv toffee noses
And Poofs in coffee houses
And Fings ain't wot they used t'be.
Short time low-priced mysteries
Wivaht proper histories,
Fings ain't wot they used t'be.
There used ter be class,
Doin' the town,
Buyin' a bit of vice.
And that's when a brass,
Couldn't go down
Under the Union price, not likely!
Once in golden days of yore
Ponces killed a lazy whore,
Fings ain't wot they used t'be.

The opening night of *Fings* heralded a new era in the history of the English theatre. Joan Littlewood described its impact: 'In the theatre of those dear departed days when every actress had roses round her vowels, and a butler's suit was an essential part of an actor's equipment, the voice of the Cockney was one long whine of blissful servitude. No play was complete without its moronic maid or faithful batman – rich with that true cockney speech and humour learned in the drama schools. Frank Norman had never seen such plays, nor even been in a theatre, when he wrote *Fings Ain't Wot They Used T'Be*. If he had he would probably have run for his life. His first venture into any theatre was at Stratford, with the first draft of his own play. With a true instinct for theatre he worked as a playwright must, in collaboration with the actors, and with Lionel Bart the composer. New ideas, arising out of rehearsal, were drafted into the text, until an entertainment was produced which packed our theatre night after night with cockney people, most of whom, like Frank Norman, had never been in a theatre in their lives.'

The theatre critics who made the seven-mile pilgrimage from the West End didn't altogether get the message. *The Stage* reported: 'It is not a

A scene from *Fings* in its West End production at the Garrick Theatre

good musical, but there are some effective songs. They show Mr Bart as a potential contributor of value to this medium of entertainment.' *Theatre World* remained unconvinced: 'Ten songs by Lionel Bart – not especially captivating in themselves – acted like explosive dumplings in the stew.'

Despite its lukewarm reception from the press, *Fings* enjoyed a two-month run at the Theatre Royal. It was revived in the autumn, and the following year moved 'Up West' to the Garrick Theatre. En route, the Lord Chamberlain – Lord Scarborough – insisted on a number of modifications. He was particularly concerned about Lionel Bart's song 'Contempery', as performed by Wallas Eaton, playing the interior decorator 'Horace Seaton' with a very limp wrist:

> *Sooner or later ev'ryone has got to go*
> *Contempery. Contempery.*
> *Soon as the paint is on the wall then you*
> *   will know.*

127

Contempery. Contempery.
In my house I've got rubber plants
and cactuses.
Believe me sir, I preaches what I practises,
For very small expenditure you too can be
Contempery.

They're changing the style at Buckingham Palace.
(Oliver Messel is full of malice)
They're painting the wall that faces the yard
Pillar box red to match the Guard
(And Alice).

Have you ever caught your builder in a gay mood,
With his paintbrush in his hand?
He'll do anything you ask him within reason,
If he thinks you understand.
There's a little spark just waiting to be
kindled
(You've been swindled up till now)
Come on have a splurge and fire his urge
And he will show you how.

The Lord Chamberlain's letter to Joan Littlewood was unequivocal: 'The interior decorator is *not* to be played as a homosexual. The line "I've strained myself" is to be omitted. The builder's labourer is *not* to carry the plank at the erotic angle he does: the Lord Chamberlain wishes to be informed of the manner in which the plank is in future to be carried.'

In 1959, the Songwriters' Guild of Great Britain gave Lionel Bart a special Ivor Novello Award for 'outstanding services to British music'. Besides *Fings*, he'd now written the lyrics for a musical at the brand-new Mermaid Theatre in the City of London – *Lock up your Daughters*: and he was still churning out hit songs for his friends – 'D'you Mind' for Tony Newley, 'Living Doll' for Cliff Richard. He was also in danger of becoming a celebrity, and acquiring a reputation among journalists for being 'difficult'. The *Sunday Dispatch* reported: 'The most successful songwriter since Ivor Novello and Noël Coward is a small, dark ex-slum-dweller with a chip on his shoulder, three cars in the garage, and an income of something like £50,000 a year. It is practically certain that some time in the past four years you have hummed or whistled a Bart melody without giving a second thought to the identity of the composer:

Keith Hamshere as Oliver Twist and Ron Moody as
Fagin in *Oliver*, as seen by Hewison in *Punch*

although envious rivals are apt to describe Bart as "dead commercial",
any of them would gladly trade their eye-teeth in exchange for his
common touch and uncommon talent. As he rubbed his nose – it's a long,
thin nose that is poised over his mouth like a permanent exclamation
mark – Mr Bart told me "Everything I do must be bigger and better than
anything I've done before. That's my kick, mate."'

True to his word, and with two of his shows still running in the West
End, Bart produced his tour-de-force. A musical on the grand scale –
book, music *and* lyrics by Lionel Bart, with a little help from Charles
Dickens. Of its sixteen songs four went straight into the Top Twenty,
and one – 'As Long as He Needs Me' – became an all-time favourite with

129

lady singers. The lavish West End production ran to a record-breaking 2618 performances – even surpassing *Chu Chin Chow*. He had a similar success on Broadway, then a feature film, and Oscars galore. It's small wonder that the first-night reception of *Oliver* was described as 'the most ecstatic London has witnessed since *Oklahoma*': or that the twenty-nine-year-old composer was seen to be 'glistening like a garden-gnome after a shower'.

In the weeks that followed, the accolades poured in. The *Sunday Times* described him as 'the first composer to have emerged fully fledged from the labyrinths of rock'n'roll'. The Songwriters' Guild presented him with *three* more Ivor Novello Awards. The Variety Club voted him 'Show Business Personality of 1960'; the Russians sent him a special diploma; and Bertrand Russell invited him to collaborate on a musical version of *Satan in Suburbia*. For all that, his parents assured *Daily Mail* reporters that success had not changed their boy in any way – except, that is, for his name and his nose, which he'd had re-shaped to suit his newly-acquired celebrity status. He also experienced his first cash-flow problem, which, luckily, coincided with a phone call from Noël Coward. Bart recalls:

'He'd been to see my show *Oliver*, and I'd had a telegram from him to say how much he'd enjoyed it. Then, about four weeks later, I was sitting in my flat in Kensington when the phone rang. Now you've got to understand that I'm the godfather of Noël Harrison (that's Rex Harrison's son). In fact, I'm a godfather forty-eight times over and an uncle thirty-five times over: so I send them all presents on *my* birthday because it's easier. But, anyway, there's this phone call. The phone goes and this voice says: "Hello, this is Noël." And I said: "Noël who?" And the voice replies, "Coward, you Cockney * * * *" – which is alliteration, right? However, he said: "I hear you've just gone broke for the first time. Pack a toothbrush and come to Switzerland." Which I did. Got there, signed the Visitor's Book, his man Coley took a snapshot of me, and I got long finger-waggings from Noël. In the end, he loaned me some money (he got it back in four weeks): and he told me all about *his* flops. He said, "Everyone has to have a flop at some time or another." And he advised me, "Never invest in your own shows, Lionel." But I didn't bide his warning. . . .'

Bart's next show owed something to Noël Coward's spectacular, *Cavalcade*. In collaboration with the stage designer Sean Kenny, he re-created the London of his own experience – the pubs, street corners, synagogues and markets of his boyhood – and inhabited by his own people, the ordinary working people of London, in the extraordinary days of the Blitz. He even recruited Vera Lynn to sing his own parody of

One of Sean Kenny's spectacular sets for *Blitz*

a 'war-time weepie' – 'The Day after Tomorrow' – which became a fairly substantial hit in its own right.

For all its nostalgic potency, and Kenny's spectacular sets, *Blitz* couldn't match the success of its three predecessors – which were all *still* going strong when *Blitz* opened in May 1962. The *Daily Express* critic described it as 'a massive disappointment, and, for at least half of its length, a bore': nevertheless he admitted that 'Bart has done so much for the British Musical, that to wish *Blitz* anything other than success would be uncharitable'.

Kenneth Haigh as Patrick Casey and Rachel Roberts in
the title role of *Maggie May* (cartoon by Hewison in *Punch*)

He needn't have worried. *Blitz* repaid its £60,000 investment in four months, and ran for eighteen. Proliferating wildly in all directions, Bart now set up his own film production company, and a music publishing house. He bought a mansion in Chelsea for £60,000 and put a fibre-glass stork on the chimney. He threw extravagant parties, and hobnobbed with the rich and famous. In October 1962, *Oliver* celebrated its 1000th performance. In two and a half years it had clocked up audiences of more than a million, including the Queen, who saw it twice; Viscount Montgomery was another enthusiast.

Meanwhile, Bart was busy preparing a new musical – although he preferred to call this one a 'folk opera'. Pressed to explain what he meant, he said: 'Well, it's a piece which will contain masses of singing and, er, it's got folk in it!' Folk music, too: indeed, the title-song of the show – 'Maggie May' – had been around for decades before Lionel Bart borrowed it. In his researches, he also discovered that most of

Tarts on the picket-lines:
a scene from *Maggie May*

Liverpool's folk music had Celtic roots: and even went on to argue that
the Liverpool Irish were the lost tribe of Israel. His collaborator, Alun
Owen, helped him to assimilate the local dialect – 'part-Irish, part-
Welsh, and part-catarrh': and Sean Kenny adapted the New Brighton
Ferry and the Pier Head to the stage of the Adelphi Theatre, where
Maggie May succeeded *Blitz* in September 1964. As always, the best
songs were those into which Bart put a lot of himself.

Although two of the songs from *Maggie May* did manage to creep into
the lower reaches of the Top Twenty, the legendary sailors' tart was no
match for the four fellow-Liverpudlians who in 1964 were well on their
way to becoming Scouse folk-heroes themselves. 'She Loves You', 'Can't
buy Me Love' and 'A Hard Day's Night' were the songs that swept the
board at the Ivor Novello Award Ceremony that year, causing some of
the more conservative members of the Songwriters' Guild to speculate
whether Ivor himself might not now be turning in his grave at the sight,

and sound, of these new inheritors of his kingdom: 'Bart was bad enough, but those Beatles! . . .'

Bart refused to see the writing on the wall. He took up Yoga, and invented a waterproof book for reading in the bath. He converted his lavatory into a panelled throne room, explaining 'I'm on a big mediaeval kick at the moment'. He bought two vast chandeliers that had been made for the film *Becket* and hung them in his drawing room. Although now earning more than £8000 a week in royalties, he refused to contemplate retirement: 'Writer-schmiter: I'm a showman . . . I can't go to a desert island – too many people need me. . . .'

For his next theatrical extravaganza, he devised a show about Robin Hood – with whom he'd always felt a certain affinity. His backers were a little apprehensive. After two near misses, they would have preferred to see Bart back on his home ground, instead of camping it up in Sherwood Forest. But the Golden Boy of British Musicals was unruffled. The successful *Fings* team was reassembled: Joan Littlewood to direct her first West End show for five years, James Booth to play Robin Hood and Barbara Windsor as Delphina. With the backing of Bernard Delfont, a first night in London was fixed for 8 December 1965, after a 'try-out' in Birmingham and Manchester.

In October, came the first intimations that all was not going according to plan. The Birmingham visit was inexplicably cancelled, and the world première of *Twang!!!* rescheduled for Manchester. Then came news that Joan Littlewood had walked out, after a backstage clash with the composer, and that only a deputation from the cast had persuaded her to carry on. From Manchester, Bernard Delfont was quoted as saying: 'I am not a very happy man.'

The first-night audience at the Palace Theatre, Manchester, stuck it out – but only just. Fifty people walked out during the closing number; there was only a smattering of applause at the final curtain, and no curtain calls for the cast. Afterwards Bart stood on the stage grasping a bottle of beer, and said: 'Now I'm going to get a grip on this show. I'm going to put my stamp on it. Joan Littlewood and I will do it together. We're going to scrap two songs, cut the show by forty-five minutes, write four new songs and get it ready for the London opening on 8 December.'

Two weeks later Joan Littlewood resigned again: and this time she stayed away. James Booth complained: 'This show has become sheer drudgery. For seven weeks I have worked fourteen hours a day without a break. It seems every line has been rewritten four times.' American writer Burt Shevelove (author of *A Funny Thing Happened. . .*) was

Hewison of *Punch* gives a satirical view of the first night of *Twang!!!*

summoned to Manchester, to reshape the show – and Bart continued to assure reporters that *Twang!!!* would open in London as planned, and that he would even be prepared to bear the cost of backing it himself.

Taking him at his word, Bernard Delfont pulled out, complaining that the show had already cost about £100,000 and to bring it into the West End would add a further £30,000 to the bill. It was left to Lionel Bart to put his money where his mouth was, and provide the financial backing for the London opening. Which he did, disregarding Noël Coward's finger-wagging advice of five years earlier. In an interview in the *Daily Sketch*, Bart confessed that he had done a ten-year deal with a film company (United Artists), signing away a major share of all his future royalties – mortgaging songs and shows that he hadn't even written. 'I've sold my body and soul,' he joked.

Unaware that Bart had staked his financial independence on *Twang!!!* the theatre critics arrived for the London first night on 20 December with knives well-sharpened. 'Oh Dear, Oh Dear,' bewailed the *Daily Mirror*, 'Fings really Ain't Wot They Used To Be.... The only

(*Overleaf*) Lionel Bart at the piano, surrounded by mementoes of his successes

memorable song up to the interval was the National Anthem.' The *Daily Mail*, under the headline CLANG – BART'S MUSICAL BOOED, noted that, at the final curtain, a voice from the gallery had shouted 'Thank God that's over!' The *Evening News* declared '*Twang!!!* It's off target': and, in the same edition, reported a last word from the composer himself ' "I still say it's a hit," says Bart.'

Thirteen years later, he still maintains that he was the victim of a conspiracy: 'If you've had seven hits, it's only news if you have a flop. Now while we'd been out of town, in Manchester and elsewhere, there were so many fracas between Joan Littlewood, Oliver Messel, Bernard Delfont, Tony Armstrong-Jones and myself, that, by the time we came into London, we were a household word – like Harpic! It wasn't news to say we were a success. So it was almost manipulated that we should become a flop.'

When *Twang!!!* collapsed after only eight days in London, the whole Bart empire folded with it. The events of the next few years are part of showbiz history: encapsulated in the headlines of the day, which positively reek of the relish with which the British popular press likes to celebrate the downfall of an upstart. December, 1965: 'TWANG SONG WRIT'. May, 1966: 'BART'S FUN-PALACE BUILDER SUES'. October, 1967: 'BART SUED FOR £36,000'. March, 1968: 'IF YOU'VE GOT £100,000 THIS MORNING, PUT IN A BID FOR BART'S HOUSE'. May, 1969: 'THIEVES RANSACK BART'S HOME'. February, 1971: 'BART ARRESTED ON DRUGS CHARGE'. March, 1972: 'BART FALLS IN STYLE'. April, 1972: 'MUSICMAN BART FACES £158,000 DEBTS'. October 1972: 'BART COMPANY WOUND UP'. November 1972: 'BART SAYS – I'M DOWN TO MY PIANO'.

Today, Lionel Bart lives in the same rented mews flat where he wrote his first song hits. On the piano is a signed photograph of Noël Coward, the silver heart of the Variety Club, and his Russian diploma. His desk-draw is full of cassettes – each one a Bart musical, as yet unproduced, unpublished, unknown. *Golda Meir, Gulliver's Travels, Limpy Lawson, The Hunchback of Notre Dame, King Lear* – all subjects currently on Bart's drawing board, in various stages of completion. His song-writing method hasn't changed: 'Usually it's the words, a line of words first and then the music comes after it. Then I build from there: I sing it into a tape, or I play it onto a piano in my own code which is not music, because I can't read or write music. I use a kind of tonic sol-fa or a basis of tonic sol-fa, which is something that I have in common with other writers like John Lennon.

'When Oscar Hammerstein died, Richard Rodgers came to see me wanting me to be his partner, you know, and we tossed around an idea about *Moll Flanders* for about a year. He came here and I went to New York, and then I said: "Look man, I usually leave holes in my songs because if they are going on the stage I like to be amazed by what's going to come off the stage and then write for the people." "Oh, I can't work like that," he said. "Oscar Hammerstein always used to bring me his lyrics engraved in concrete as it were." And I said, "What, you just wrote tunes to them?" And he said, "Yes." I said, "Okay, here's a lyric," which I just wrote there and then; and he sat down at the piano in his office and did a Richard Rodgers tune, which was totally new and original but was unmistakeably a Richard Rodgers tune. And I said, "Look, goodness me, you've worked with the best lyric writer of the decade, of the century – Lorenz Hart – and you need me like a hole in the head, you know." And I talked him into writing his own lyrics – which in fact he did. He wrote a show called *No Strings* for Diahann Carroll, in which there was one extremely good song called "The Sweetest Sounds I Ever Heard"....

'The secret of a hit song is, I suppose, that people know the next note coming up, and almost the next word coming up. But you surprise them here and there with the wrong word and the wrong note. Then you get back to what they feel familiar with. But it's not studied – it's instinctive, isn't it really?

'When you *want* to do it, you do it. And when you *have* to do it, you do it. At the moment I don't have to or want to.'

JOHN LENNON &
PAUL McCARTNEY

'A Hard Day's Night'

On 4 November 1963 Leicester Square was overrun by hordes of screaming teenage girls. Marlene Dietrich had some difficulty fighting her way to the stage door of the Prince of Wales Theatre, where she was due to rehearse for that night's Royal Variety Performance. At seven o'clock, when the Queen Mother accompanied by Princess Margaret and Lord Snowdon arrived, they were greeted by shouts of 'We want the Beatles!' On stage, four young men with identical pudding-basin haircuts and shiny, high-collar suits, sang 'Please, Please Me' to a respectful, though undemonstrative, adult audience. Then one of the guitarists, John Lennon, stepped to the front of the stage. 'On this next number,' he said, 'I want you all to join in. Would those in the cheap seats clap their hands? The rest of you can rattle your jewellery.' Afterwards, in the royal lounge, the four Beatles were introduced to the Queen Mother. She told them that she had enjoyed the show, and asked where they would be performing next. At Slough, they told her. 'Ah,' she said with obvious delight, 'that's near us.' Beatlemania had received the royal imprimatur.

The explosive force which projected the Beatles so precipitately onto the national consciousness is without precedent in the history of British popular music. '1963 – THE YEAR OF THE BEATLES' headlined the *Evening Standard*, reporting that 'an examination of the heart of the nation at this moment would reveal the word BEATLES engraved upon it.' Over the next five years, the Beatles tightened their hold on the decade, projecting their image into aspects of contemporary life from the ridiculous ('Swinging London') to the sublime (Transcendental Meditation), while providing, in the songs of Lennon and McCartney, a perpetual lyrical accompaniment to the tempo of the Sixties.

The first collection of Lennon and McCartney songs to be released on record was an EP containing 'Please, Please Me', 'Love Me Do', 'From Me to You', and 'Thank You Girl'. It made an ideal stocking-filler for Christmas 1963. A perspicacious publicist at Parlophone Records, Tony Barrow, wrote the accompanying sleeve-note: 'The four numbers on this EP have been selected from the Lennon and McCartney Songbook. If that description sounds a trifle pompous, I suggest you preserve this sleeve for about ten years, then exhume it from your collection and write me a very nasty letter if the pop people of the Seventies aren't talking, *with respect*, about these titles being "early examples of Modern Beat Standards taken from the Lennon and McCartney Songbook".' He was right, of course. They did. George Melly, *Revolt into Style* (1971):

> 'The first compositions of Lennon and McCartney fulfilled one of the essential conditions of a pop single: to sound like every other pop song and yet somehow to lodge in the mind like a burr. Yet, while both in imagery and musical idiom the early songs seemed to break no new ground, it soon became clear that they were both superior to and different from the run-of-the-mill pop tunes of their period. If you try and recollect the other numbers in the hit parade at the same time as 'Love Me Do' or 'I Want To Hold Your Hand', there is confirmation of this assumption. What's more the words, while seemingly mere cliché, proved extraordinarily accurate in reflecting the language and attitude of a whole generation of teenagers. These songs were not *about* Liverpool; that area was to be explored later when the Beatles had left – emotion recollected in turmoil; but they trapped what it felt like to be a rebellious suburban Liverpudlian for whom beat music offered an escape. They were tough *and* tender. You could sense, behind the words and music, the emergence of a new spirit: post-war, clever, nonconformist, and above all cool.'

The 'rebellious suburban Liverpudlian' was already one jump ahead of his contemporaries in Glasgow, Birmingham and London. The city's close ties with America – a legacy from the great days of the cotton trade – provided, in the mid-Fifties, a direct link to the true source of the rock 'n' roll explosion, on the other side of the Atlantic. The 'Ted' culture that surrounded rock 'n' roll depended largely on America for its style and imagery – sneakers and sideburns, Lucky Strike and James Dean. And the Americanisms in all this were never more evident than in the seaport of Liverpool. Whereas the kids in most other parts of the country had to make do with black-and-white reprints of Superman comics, Woolworths baseball boots and Western shirts made in Manchester, in Liverpool there was a chance of getting your hands on the real thing. Everyone had a big brother, or knew someone who had a big brother, in

Rehearsal for the Royal Variety
Performance of 1963. The Beatles line
up with Marlene Dietrich and Tommy Steele

the Merchant Navy. Those that didn't would probably end up at sea
anyway. In a town that depended on the seasonal variations of the
docks, full employment was unknown, and for a whole generation of
working-class youngsters, after National Service was abolished, the
only viable alternative to the dole was the 'Merch'.

So emerged the 'Cunard Yanks': the lads that worked the Cunard and
Blue Star lines to New York and the eastern seaboard down to New
Orleans. And they were the lads to contact if you wanted anything in the
way of American ciggies, clothes, or records. It was the supply, in this
way, of otherwise unavailable records that proved the most significant
part of this strange transatlantic export of a sub-culture. Even at the
height of the mid-Fifties rock 'n' roll madness the record companies only
released the most obviously commercial material from the States. While
Elvis and Bill Haley grew rich on their English royalties, black music –

John Lennon and the Quarrymen, June 1955

the original 'rhythm and blues' – was only available to those who could get it direct. This situation got worse towards the end of the decade, as Tin Pan Alley began to back-pedal away from solid rock 'n' roll, and turn to a goo of Bobby Vee and Shadows imitators. At this time there were no shops in Britain selling imported records, so the consequence of the 'Cunard Yank' trade was that there was a whole wealth of material fairly easily available in Liverpool that simply wasn't to be found elsewhere.

Interviewed in 1970, John Lennon recalled: 'We felt that the message was "Listen to this music!" We felt very exclusive and underground in Liverpool, listening to all those old-time records: Chuck Berry and the blues singers, the really funky black music. And nobody else was listening to them except Eric Burdon in Newcastle and Mick Jagger in London. It was that lonely. . . .'

John Lennon was born in Liverpool, during an air-raid, on 9 October 1940. His father, Fred Lennon, was a 'Cunard Yank', with a good ear for music. He taught John's mother, Julia, how to play the banjo. They separated soon after John was born, and from the age of five, he was brought up by his Auntie Mimi. As a boy, he was tough, independent, aggressive. He hated school, although he loved reading books, and started writing his own stories when he was seven. His first musical instrument was a mouth-organ, given to him by a friendly bus conductor. Then he got a guitar, and formed a skiffle group with friends from his school, Quarry Bank High.

Paul McCartney was born in Liverpool on 18 June 1942. His father had been a 'semi-pro' musician, who used to play the piano in a ragtime band called 'The Masked Melody Makers'. His mother was a midwife. At school, Paul was quiet, studious, diplomatic. He passed the Eleven Plus without much effort, and went to the Liverpool Institute. When he was fourteen, his mother died, and soon after this he asked his father to buy him a guitar, which cost £15. The guitar became an obsession: he had no time for homework, meals or football – he played it on the lavatory, in the bath, everywhere. His father tried to steer him towards the good old tunes like 'Stairway to Paradise' and 'When the Saints Go Marching In' – but it was too late. Paul had already sold his soul to rock 'n' roll. 'It was a really electric atmosphere,' he recalls. 'For once the kids had something which the grown-ups couldn't – or didn't want to – share. That gave it a real magic feeling.'

Paul McCartney met John Lennon for the first time at a Church fête in the summer of 1956. John was providing the music with his group, the Quarrymen. Paul said: 'They weren't bad. They played things like 'Maggie May' but with the words a bit different. John had made them up himself, as he didn't know the right ones. I went round to see them afterwards. I showed them how to play 'Twenty Flight Rock' and did my Little Richard impression. I remember this beery old man getting nearer and breathing down my neck as I was playing. It was John. He'd just had a few beers. He was 16 and I was 14, so he was a big man. I showed him how to play a few more chords he didn't know. Then I left. I felt I'd made an impression.'

He had. John said: 'It was obvious that Paul knew how to play the guitar. I half thought to myself – "He's as good as me." I'd been kingpin up to then. "Now", I thought, "if I take him on, what'll happen?" But he was good, so he was worth having.' They got to know one another. They stayed away from school, and spent the afternoons at Paul's house, eating fried eggs and listening to records: Chuck Berry, Ray Charles, Little Richard. Paul had written some songs of his own, which he played to John. Not to be outdone, John immediately started writing some of his own stuff. And they started helping one another out – suggesting a new line or a different chord for the song that was emerging from the hours of guitar-doodling and word-juggling. By the time they left school, they'd filled an exercise book with Lennon and McCartney compositions.

In the autumn of 1957, John went to Art College. He didn't enjoy it – he wanted to do illustrations, but the instructors made him do lettering. The following summer, his mother was knocked down in the street, not far from Auntie Mimi's house. Although John hadn't lived with his mother for twelve years, they had remained close, and her death had a profound effect on him. As he recalled: 'I was in a sort of blind range for two years. I was either drunk or fighting.' His girlfriend, Cynthia Powell, who was in the same class at college, thought he was horrible: 'He looked awful in those days. He had this long tweed overcoat which had belonged to his Uncle George, and his hair greased back. I didn't fancy him at all at first. He was outrageous: he used to come out with things that other people would be too scared to say. He was cruel. Walking down the street he would shout "Boo" at old people. Or if he saw anyone who was crippled or deformed, he'd say, "Some people will do anything to get out of the army." John had a complete disrespect for everything. But he always had an audience round him.'

At lunch time, John and Paul used to practise their guitar-playing in the college hall. Other friends joined them occasionally: Eddie Clayton, George Harrison, and Stuart Sutcliffe, who couldn't play an instrument but was very keen to join the group. They began to make a name for themselves, and were invited to play at friends' parties, social clubs and church functions – occasionally earning as much as 15/- a night each. They played under a different name every night. Since John had left school 'The Quarrymen' was inappropriate, and the boys couldn't agree on a replacement. They introduced the group with new names, sometimes invented on the spur of the moment – 'Johnny and The Moondogs', 'The Rainbows'.

The problem was still unresolved when, in 1959, Paul McCartney wrote to a journalist they'd met in a pub, and who had expressed an interest in the group. He wrote:

Dear Mr Low,

    I am sorry about the time I have taken to write to you, but I hope I have not left it too late. Here are some details about the group. It consists of four boys: Paul McCartney (guitar), John Lennon (guitar), Stuart Sutcliffe (bass) and George Harrison (another guitar) and is called. . . . This line-up may at first seem rather dull but it must be appreciated that as the boys have above-average instrumental ability they achieve surprisingly varied effects. Their basic beat is off-beat, but this has recently tended to be accompanied by a faint on-beat; thus the overall sound is rather reminiscent of the four-in-the-bar of traditional jazz. This could possibly be put down to the influence of Mr McCartney who led one of the top local jazz bands ('Jim Mac's Jazz Band') in the 1930s. Modern music is, however, the group's delight, and as if to prove the point, John and Paul have written over fifty tunes, ballads and faster numbers, during the last three years.

The boys got their first glimpse of the big time soon after this, when they auditioned for the great Larry Parnes, and were booked for a two-week tour of Scotland, backing a singer called Johnny Gentle. En route, they acquired a name. According to John:

'A man appeared on a flaming pie and said unto them "From this day on you are BEATLES with an A". "Thank you, Mister Man," they said, thanking him.
'And then a man with a beard cut off said "Will you go to Germany (Hamburg) and play mighty rock for the peasants for money?" And we said we would play mighty anything for money. But before we could go, we had to grow a drummer, so we grew one in West Kirby and his trouble was Pete Best. We called "Hello Pete: come off to Germany!" "Yes!" ZOOOOOOOOOOOOOOOOOOM!'

Hamburg is Germany's Liverpool. It's a large Northern port. The inhabitants are rough and tough, but underneath they can be soft and sentimental. The climate is wet and windy. The two towns share the same latitude, 53 degrees North.

The Beatles hit Hamburg in April 1960. They arrived by mini-van, having stopped off in Holland to let John do some shoplifting. They were booked to play in a grotty basement club called the Indra. At first, they got a pretty cool reception. Then the manager told them that they ought to 'Mach Schau' – 'Make a Show' – like the group down the road were doing. So they did. John said:

'We were a bit scared by it all at first, being in the middle of that tough clubland. But we felt cocky, coming from Liverpool, at least believing the myth about Liverpool producing cocky people. In Hamburg we had to play for eight hours every night, so we really had to find a new way of playing. We played very loud, bang, bang, all the time. And we all did Mach Schauing – jumping around, rolling on the floor. The Germans loved it. We got better, and got more confidence. We couldn't help it, with all the experience, playing all night long. It was handy there, being foreign. We had to try even harder, put our heart and soul into it, to get ourselves over.'

The Beatles made few friends in Hamburg. But they did acquire two faithful fans: art student Klaus Voormann, and his girl-friend Astrid Kirchner. Astrid took photographs of the Beatles, and advised them to

Paul, John and George on a roof in Hamburg, 1961

change their hair-style from greasy Teddy-boy 'duck's back', to the well-washed mop that became their trade-mark.

After Hamburg, the Beatles hit Liverpool like a tornado. When they played at Litherland Town Hall, the audience went mad. Some of the kids thought that they were a German group: their wild, noisy antics on stage were unlike anything that had been seen or heard before. A far-sighted Liverpool DJ, Bob Wooller, saw what was happening that night. In *Mersey Beat*, he wrote later:

'The Beatles hit the scene when it had been emasculated by figures like Cliff Richard and sounds like those electronic wonders, The Shadows, and their many imitators. Gone was the drive that inflamed emotions. This was studio music, purveyed skilfully in a chartwise direction by arrangement with the record companies' A & R men.

'The Beatles, therefore, exploded onto a jaded scene. And for those people on the verge of quitting teendom – those who had experienced during their most impressionable years the impact of rhythm and blues music (now rock 'n' roll) – this was an experience, a process of regaining and re-living a style of sounds and associated feelings identifiable with their era. Here again, in the Beatles, was the stuff that screams are made of. Here was the excitement – both physical and aural – that symbolised the rebellion of youth in the ennuied mid-Fifties. This was the real thing.'

The group was paid £6 for the Litherland Town Hall gig. John said: 'It was that evening that we really came out of our shell and let go. This was when we began to think that we were good. Up to Hamburg, we'd thought that we were OK, but not good enough.'

The crowds followed the Beatles, and most evenings ended in a riot. They played at The Cavern Club – previously an exclusive haunt of jazz-men, who viewed the rock 'n' roll explosion with great foreboding. There was no love lost on either side. 'We were always anti-jazz', said John Lennon in 1971. 'I think it is shit music, followed by students in Marks and Spencer pullovers. Jazz never gets anywhere, never does anything, it's all the same and all they do is drink pints of beer. We hated it because in the early days they wouldn't let us play at those sort of clubs. We'd never get auditions because of the jazz bands.'

It was at The Cavern that Brian Epstein, manager of a Liverpool record shop, heard the Beatles and offered to represent them, for a 25% cut. He persuaded George Martin at Parlophone Records to give them an audition, and a contract. In September 1962, by which time they had acquired a new drummer – Ringo Starr – the group recorded their first single, 'Love Me Do'. It was a Lennon and McCartney composition: it took them seventeen takes to record it, and it went to number 17 in the hit parade.

'Love Me Do' dated from John and Paul's schoolboy collaboration. In fact, it's the only one of those early songs that they thought worth recording: by now they were writing new stuff, and although George Martin tried to persuade them to record other writers' songs, they stuck to their guns. Their second release, 'Please Please Me', went to number one.

In February 1963 the Beatles went on a nationwide tour; but as the supporting act for Helen Shapiro. In March, they played second fiddle to Chris Montez. In May, they were top of the bill for the first time, with Roy Orbison, and Gerry and the Pacemakers in support. On tour, John and Paul wrote new songs every day. On the coach, in Yorkshire, they produced the song which launched the second phase of the Lennon and McCartney partnership. It was also one of the last songs they wrote together: 'She Loves You'.

More than fifteen million people, including the Queen, saw the

Brian Epstein photographed with the Beatles
during a break in television filming

Beatles sing 'She Loves You' on television. The pundits had a field-day. Music critic of *The Times*, William Mann, wrote: 'Lennon and McCartney have brought a distinctive and exhilarating flavour into a genre of music that was in danger of ceasing to be music at all. The autocratic but not by any means ungrammatical attitude to tonality; the exhilarating and often quasi-instrumental vocal duetting; the melismas with altered vowels ("I saw her yesterday-ee-ay") which have not quite become mannered; the translation of African Blues and American western idioms into tough, sensitive Merseyside – these are some of the qualities which make one wonder with interest what Lennon and McCartney will do next. . . .'

At York University, Professor Wilfrid Mellers based a series of lectures on the music of the Beatles. Of 'She Loves You', he said: 'It is quintessential. It exists in the moment, without before or after. For although its key signature is the E flat beloved of Tin Pan Alley, the opening phrase is pentatonic, or perhaps an Aeolian C which veers

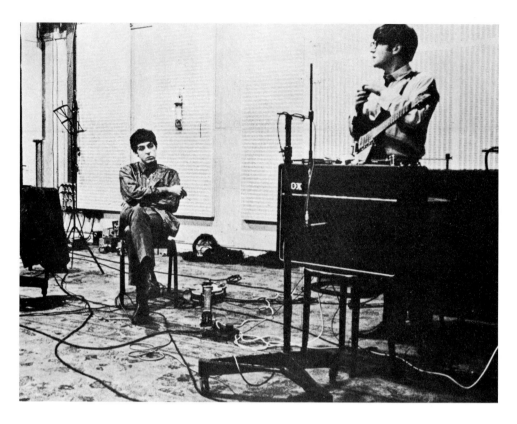

The Lennon-McCartney partnership takes a break in the recording studios

towards E flat. The timeless, present-affirming modality is instinctive: the Beatles are, through their music, as if new-born. It's this pristine quality that helps us to understand the potency of their appeal.'

The *Daily Mirror* put it another way: 'Yeah! Yeah! Yeah! You have to be a real sour square not to love the nutty, noisy, happy, handsome Beatles. If they don't sweep your blues away – brother, you're a lost cause. If they don't put a beat in your feet – sister, you're not living.'

At London Airport, on their return from a Swedish concert, the Fab Four encountered the full force of Beatlemania for the first time. Thousands of screaming fans lined the roof of the terminal building. In the ensuing chaos, the car containing the Prime Minister, Sir Alec Douglas-Home, was completely ignored. These airport scenes became familiar over the next two years, during which the group became public property, rivalling even the Royal Family for public interest, worship, ridicule, love and hate. Denied any privacy, or liberty, they spent their lives running from dressing-room to limousine to hotel to airport. John Lennon described it as 'Fellini's *Satyricon* with four musicians going through it.'

Their refuge was the recording studio: and it was *here* that the Lennon and McCartney partnership really flourished. Shut away from the world, and turned in on themselves, they created a new world in their songs: a world of the imagination – a weird and wonderful place concocted out of dreams, childhood memories, fantasy and foreboding. The songs that they wrote between 1964 and 1969 are on a different plane from the direct rock 'n' roll numbers that they cut their teeth on. Nor do these later songs have anything in common with the romantic generalities of the standard pop song. If they have a common theme, it's loneliness.

It's from this point that the separate personalities of Lennon and McCartney become apparent in their songs. Though they never jointly wrote another song, they continued to work together, because they enjoyed it: egging one another on, and learning from one another, as they had done when they were schoolboys. And while they continued to share the credit for one another's work, you can detect in every song the voice of its author. John, the Liverpool hard man with a soft centre, the joker, the extrovert. He's the one crying for 'HELP – I need somebody': he's the Nowhere Man, the Walrus. Paul's voice is more lyrical, wistful. He tells sad stories of lost and lonely people – Eleanor Rigby, Lady Madonna, the Fool on the Hill.

It's a strange collaboration. They produced their best songs when they were working together – and yet they were never really that close. John said of their first encounter: 'Meeting Paul was just like two people meeting: not falling in love or anything – just us.'

The later Lennon and McCartney songs tell their own story – whether in flashback to the Liverpool streets of their childhood, in oblique reference to the events surrounding them, or in drug-induced hallucination. What is remarkable is that such very *personal* songs should have become so universally popular. The Tin Pan Alley professional makes his song as unspecific as possible, in the hope that millions the world over will relate to his basic theme. The soppy love song thus becomes the lowest common denominator. Lennon and McCartney make no such concessions: the listener must come more than halfway to meet them, and find his own, individual response to what he hears.

John Lennon made the same voyage of discovery in his teens: 'Rock 'n' roll was the only thing to get through to me after all the things that were happening to me when I was fifteen. Rock 'n' roll was real – everything else was unreal. Realism gets through to you, despite yourself. You recognize something in it which is true, like all true art,

whatever art is. If it's real, it's simple usually, and if it's simple, it's true – something like that. Rock 'n' roll got through to you finally.'

Paul McCartney finds it more difficult to analyse what was going on: 'It's nothing you can talk about really. Music isn't words: if you can talk about it, then it wouldn't be music. It's like it comes in out of the blue – the funnel that it's coming through is what's important. But I've always felt that it wasn't *me* doing it: like, one morning I just fell out of bed with the tune of 'Yesterday' in my head. Although it did take me some time to find the words to go with the tune: for weeks I went around singing 'scrambled egg' to the first three notes of the tune.'

'Yesterday' became Paul McCartney's 'bread-and-butter' song. To date, it's been recorded by more than 200 different artists, including the Big Ben Banjo Band, and the Irish Guards: and it provides, for both Paul *and* John, a substantial annual income from royalties. In fact, if the partners *had* decided to identify their songs individually, and collect royalties accordingly, Paul would be a wealthier man than John today. His particular gift for melody, and relatively more accessible ideas have made his songs more popular with singers and musicians: 'Yesterday', 'Michelle', 'Hey Jude', and 'Lady Madonna' are all now well established in the 'Evergreen' section of the popular music catalogue. John Lennon's work has never made much impact in this corner of the market: 'Revolution', 'I am the Walrus', 'Glass Onion', and 'Across the Universe' are very personal songs, and the definitive vocal version remains the author's.

On the Beatles albums, Paul and John each took the lead vocal on their own songs, and, in the beginning, the identity of the singer provided listeners with the only clue as to 'who wrote what'. Soon, as faithful listeners became more familiar with the separate facets of the Lennon and McCartney partnership, the identification game became too easy. Nobody needed to be told that John's was the voice crying 'Don't Let Me Down', or that the gentle serenade to 'Michelle – ma belle' was a typical McCartney love-song.

Occasionally, their separate trajectories allowed them to come sufficiently close to one another to share an idea. Paul had a sad little story about a spinster, which he couldn't get right. Even when he changed her name from Daisy Hawkins to Eleanor Rigby, the song was still incomplete: and it was John who provided the last verse – 'Eleanor Rigby died, and was buried along with her name . . .' The same album ('Revolver') finds John exploring new planes of experience, and inviting the listener to 'turn off your mind, relax, and float downstream . . .'

Apparently inspired by a conversation with Peter Fonda, who told John that he knew what it felt like to be dead, 'Tomorrow Never Knows' uses droning sitars, chanted mantras, and backward-running tapes to create the musical equivalent of a drug-induced 'trip'. In later years, he described the effect of drugs on his music: 'It was only another mirror, it wasn't a miracle. It was more of a visual thing, and a therapy – that "looking at yourself" bit. It did all that. But it didn't *write* the music. *I* write the music, in the circumstances I'm in, whether it's on acid, or in the water. And I've always needed a drug to survive . . . I've been on pills since I was seventeen – since I became a musician. The only way to survive in Hamburg when we were playing eight hours a night was to take pills. The waiters gave you them, the pills and the drink. The others took them too, but I always had more. I always took more pills – more of everything – because I'm more crazy probably.'

Paul was the last of the four to experiment with LSD. He said: 'The taking of drugs expands the consciousness. But it's like taking an aspirin without the headache.'

The 'expanded consciousness' colours John's picture of Strawberry Fields, which was released back-to-back with Paul's 'Penny Lane' – a joint trip down memory lane to the Liverpool of their childhood. 'Let me take you down 'cos I'm going to Strawberry Fields,' sang John, reliving his visits to summer fêtes at the forbidding Victorian mansion which the Salvation Army used as an orphanage. For John, the regeneration has an eerie, lower-depths quality, emphasised by the sickening slide in the music which echoes the descent to Strawberry Fields where 'nothing is real'. On the other side, Paul paints a cheerful picture of the Penny Lane shopping centre 'underneath a blue suburban sky', peopled with quaintly surreal, Lowryesque characters – a banker with a motor-car, a barber showing photographs, a fireman with an hour-glass.

The Penny Lane/Strawberry Fields single was released in February 1967. Unlike its four predecessors it failed to reach Number One in the Top Twenty, causing the inevitable speculation that the Beatles were now past their peak. As if to force the musical press to eat its words, three months later, at a cost of £40,000, the Beatles produced their new album. On the cover, the quartet appeared moustachioed, in brightly-coloured uniforms, against a photographic assembly of celebrities from Oscar Wilde to W. C. Fields. This cover was to provoke almost as much speculation and examination as the new Lennon and McCartney songs – especially when it was noticed that the flower bed at the bottom of the picture included a thriving cannabis plant.

'Sergeant Pepper's Lonely Hearts Club Band' is a landmark in the history of the gramophone record. It sold $2\frac{1}{2}$ million copies in the first two weeks of its release: many of these have been preserved, well-worn, to this day. Anyone who was musically-conscious in 1967 can quote lines from their favourite songs: from 'Lucy in the Sky with Diamonds' (based on a drawing by John's seven-year-old son Julian, and *not* the well-known noxious substance), 'When I'm Sixty-Four' (a ragtime tribute from Paul to his father), 'With a Little Help from My Friends', 'Lovely Rita' and 'She's Leaving Home'.

The finale is a song to which both John and Paul contributed. In fact, it's two songs joined together. John's had no middle, and Paul's had no beginning: so the two bits were fused together to make 'A Day in the Life'. The opening section, by John, was inspired by real news stories which he was reading in a copy of the *Daily Mail*, propped up on the piano:

> *I read the news today, oh boy,*
> *About a lucky man who made the grade.*
> *And though the news was rather sad,*
> *Well I just had to laugh,*
> *I saw the photograph.*
> *He blew his mind out in a car . . .*

When he'd written the first section, John played it to Paul. 'I said to him, "What we want now is a middle eight bars". He said "What about this?" and sang me a song he'd written on his own, with no idea of what I was working on:

> *Woke up, fell out of bed,*
> *Dragged a comb across my head.*
> *Found my way downstairs and drank a cup*
> *And looking up I noticed I was late.*
> *Found my coat and grabbed my hat,*
> *Made the bus in seconds flat.*
> *Found my way upstairs and had a smoke.*
> *Somebody spoke and I went into a dream.*

I said "Yeah, that's it". Then we thought we needed some sort of connection bit, a growing bit to lead us back into the first bit. Like all our songs, it didn't become an entity until the very end.'

The last line of the song – 'I'd love to turn you on' – provoked BBC Radio to ban it from the air-waves, on the grounds of its 'overt drug allusions'. Professor Mellers at York University probed deeper, and

The sleeve of 'Sergeant Pepper's Lonely Hearts Club Band'
gave rise to much speculation among Beatles theorists

discovered that 'the song comes out as at once richly comic and deeply
melancholic, agitating nerves that we hardly knew we possessed. It's
the Beatles' deepest exploration of their familiar illusion-reality theme;
for them "the tragedy" is simultaneously terrifying (in a personal sense)
and grotesque (as an item in a newspaper, with a picture that almost
makes you laugh).'

At the Massachusetts Institute of Technology, Professor Langton
Winner declared: 'The closest Western civilisation has come to unity
since the congress of Vienna in 1815, was the week the "Sergeant Pepper"
album was released. In every city in Europe and America, the stereo
systems and the radio played "Lucy in the Sky with Diamonds", and

The Maharishi among his famous devotees, during a retreat
at his academy of Transcendental Meditation in the Himalayas

everyone listened. For a brief while, the irreparably fragmented consciousness of the West was unified, at least in the minds of the young.'

As if to prove their cosmic influence, in June 1967, the Beatles appeared on world-wide television, singing to an audience estimated at 150 million. The message they preached was a simple one – 'All you need is love' – although the possibility remains that the author of that song (John Lennon) might have allowed the tip of his tongue to approach the corner of his cheek. In search of divine guidance, all four Beatles headed for Bangor, North Wales, to sit at the feet of the Maharishi Mahesh Yogi. Their meditations were interrupted by news of the death of their manager, friend and mentor, Brian Epstein, from an accidental overdose. It was the end of a chapter.

In December, the Beatles formed the Apple Corporation, to handle their business affairs, and opened the Apple Shop in Baker Street. They tried their hand at film-making, and produced the Magical Mystery Tour. The film flopped, but the songs flourished: Paul's haunting 'Fool on the Hill' and John's surrealistic 'I am the Walrus', which provoked his followers into ecstasies of analytical dissection. The composer himself claimed to be totally ignorant of the meaning of the song. As a child, he'd used the same device to prevent Auntie Mimi from reading his poetry: the more sentimental thoughts were written in a carefully-executed gobbledegook which could only be deciphered by the author himself.

In 1968, John Lennon fell in love with Yoko Ono. For the first time, the unity of the group, and the fragile ties holding the Lennon and McCartney partnership together, were threatened. The first solo album by a Beatle appeared: John and Yoko's 'Two Virgins', and featuring the couple naked on the cover. 'We started the album at midnight', said John, 'and finished it at dawn. Then we made love. It was very beautiful.'

The new Beatles album, which was released at the same time, had a plain white cover. It features Paul McCartney at his chirpiest: rocking through 'Back in the USSR', foxtrotting through 'Honey Pie' and 'Rocky Racoon', and serenading his dog in 'Martha, my Dear'. John Lennon, on the other hand, uses the 'White Album' to complain 'I'm so tired, I haven't slept a wink, I'm so tired, my mind is on the blink.' He points a thinly-veiled accusing finger at the Maharishi: 'Sexy Sadie, what have you done? You made a fool of everyone.' And he has a message for Paul, in 'Glass Onion':

I told you all about the Walrus and me, man
You know that we're as close as can be, man,
Well here's another clue for you all,
The Walrus was Paul,
Standing on a cast-iron shore, yeah,
Lady Madonna trying to make ends meet, yeah,
Looking through a glass onion . . .

Some years later, John Lennon provided a footnote to the song: 'At that time, I was still in my love cloud with Yoko. I thought, "Well, I'll just say something nice to Paul, that it's all right, and you did a good job over these few years, holding us together." And he was trying to organise the group, and do the music, and be an individual artist, and all that, so I wanted to say something to him and I did it for that reason. I thought, "Well, he can have it. I've got Yoko, so thank you, you can have the credit."'

The split was widening. In February 1969 the Apple Press office announced: 'The Beatles have asked Mr Allen Klein of New York to look into their legal affairs.' At the same time, New York lawyers, Eastman and Eastman were invited to become legal consultants to Apple.

In March, Paul McCartney married Linda Eastman at Marylebone Registry Office. The following week, John Lennon and Yoko Ono were married on the Rock of Gibraltar. John changed his name to John Ono Lennon, and embarked with his new bride on a series of international 'lie-ins' for peace.

In September, the Beatles' 'Abbey Road' album was released. Beatle-ologists were quick to spot that on the cover, which showed the four Beatles in single file on a zebra crossing, Paul McCartney was out of step *and* barefoot. It was rumoured that he was dead; in fact, he was very much alive, and the dominant creative force on the album, writing most of the second side: 'Mean Mr Mustard', 'Golden Slumbers', 'She Came in Through the Bathroom Window', and 'You Never Give Me Your Money'.

That same week, John and Yoko were arrested for possessing cannabis. In November, John returned his MBE 'with love' to the Queen, in protest against Britain's involvement in Biafra and Vietnam. The Eastmans took over Northern Songs, and Paul McCartney tried to persuade the other Beatles to put all their affairs in the hands of his in-laws. John Lennon wrote to Sir Joseph Lockwood, chairman of EMI: 'Dear Sir Joe, From now on, Allen Klein handles all my stuff.'

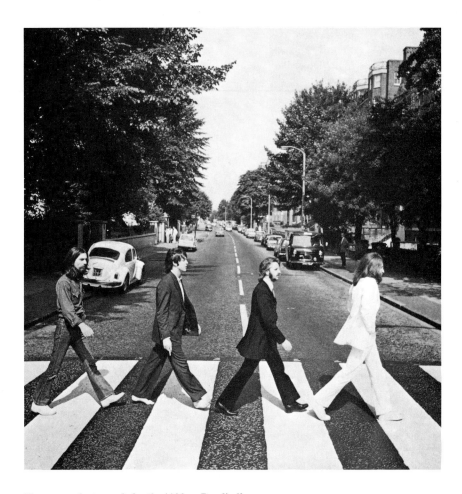

The cover-photograph for the 'Abbey Road' album

1970 ushered in a year of acrimony, insinuations, and civil litigation involving, among others, George Martin, Phil Spector, Allen Klein, Lee and John Eastman, Apple, NEMS, Triumph Investment Trust, Dick James, Northern Songs, ATV and EMI. By Christmas, it was all over. Paul answered a phone call from John with a curt 'speak to my lawyer': on 30 December, he started legal proceedings against the other three Beatles. The album 'Let it Be' had been released in May. Though recorded before 'Abbey Road' it now acquired a spurious cachet as being the 'last fruit' of the Lennon and McCartney collaboration – although the *New Musical Express* described it as 'a cheapskate epitaph, a cardboard tombstone, a sad and tatty end to a musical fusion which wiped clean and drew again the face of pop music'. The film version of 'Let it Be' captures their final fling, in a wintry open-air session on the roof of the Apple building, echoing to the sound of Paul McCartney's last rousing exhortation: 'Get back! Get back! Get back to where you once belonged!'

At the end of the song, the lugubrious voice of John Lennon can be heard, expressing the hope that the group and himself 'have passed the audition'. They had, with a vengeance. Ray Connolly, in his introduction to 'The Beatles Complete' (1970), writes: 'During the last decade pop music became more than a tawdry little industry governed by the laws of greatest profit. It became the foremost means of expression of poetry in contemporary life: it opened up a colourful world of billowing images; it enhanced the language of the young. For that we can largely thank the Beatles. The Lennon and McCartney partnership may have ended, but their work will be preserved in every home that has a record-player. The dream may be over, but it will not be forgotten . . .'

They went their separate ways: John to New York, Paul to the Outer Hebrides, George to Bangladesh, and Ringo to Weybridge. The world waited anxiously, to see if, individually, they might produce anything to compare with the extraordinary output of the Beatles years. Paul McCartney's 'Wings' took off, after a sticky start, and created a flurry of interest. But even his most devoted followers were disappointed with the new songs that came from their middle-aged hero. The Scottish sea-mists, it was feared, had dampened his creative spark: from discos across the land came the dirge-like drone of 'Mull of Kintyre', chanted by thousands of mournful teeny-boppers, who didn't know what they had missed. On the roll-call of the World's Best-Selling Artists (1970–1975), Paul McCartney was placed thirteenth, Ringo Starr fifty-first, and George Harrison seventy-second. John Lennon doesn't figure at all. The caravan is moving on, and new Superstars are Glittering on the horizon.

TIM RICE &
ANDREW LLOYD WEBBER

'Heaven On Their Minds'

Like a drunken reveller unaware of the passing of time, the 'Swinging Sixties' spilled over into the first years of the new decade – which seemed to be having some difficulty in finding a style of its own. 'The Sixties were clutter, the Seventies are empty' declared Andy Warhol, as he shuffled offstage with his fellow trendsetters – Quant, Sassoon, and Biba. The Beatles, too, showed a perfect sense of timing by bowing out at the end of their adopted decade, leaving a musical vacuum which the new generation of singer/songwriters – Marc Bolan, Gilbert O'Sullivan, Leo Sayer, Elton John – were not yet equipped to fill. A mood of desperation seized Tin Pan Alley: disc-jockeys started re-cycling the hits of previous years, creating in the 'Golden Hour' and 'Blast from the Past' a new and unwelcome phenomenon – 'short-term nostalgia' – in which even the early hits of the Beatles were being re-issued, as period curiosities, only five or six years from the date of their first hearing. 'If it's old, it must be good' reasoned the pundits, dredging even further into the musical past, to fish out other musical styles that might profitably be revived.

On television, 'The Good Old Days' resurrected the songs of the Victorian music-hall in a hotch-potch of period detail, but without the sincerity, passion and fire of the original: while the 'Black and White Minstrels' mocked the ghost of Eugene Stratton's wistful balladeer. Thirties-style dance bands flourished – The Temperance Seven, The Pasadena Roof Orchestra – with all the art deco trimmings; while in the theatre, the only musical shows to 'fill the plush' were revivals – of Kern's *Showboat, No, No, Nanette*, and even *The Maid of the Mountains* which returned to the West End on the fiftieth anniversary of its opening.

The 'English Musical', it seemed, had had its day; and some laid the blame for its demise at the door of the Beatles, who, with George Martin, had pioneered the development of the LP as an alternative showcase for a substantial musical work – without any of the hazards of the 'live' performance. This in turn raised the possibility of an album being used as a 'try-out' for a stage musical – to gauge the audience response to the material, and thereby take some of the risk out of the monumentally-expensive theatrical production that would – if the omens looked good – follow on. This theory was soon to be put into practice, with startingly successful results.

The story begins in September 1969, when two young English song-writers, Tim Rice and Andrew Lloyd Webber, approached MCA Records with a title song for a musical show that they hadn't yet written – 'Jesus Christ, Superstar'. The wheels were set in motion, and in November the song was released as a single, sung by Murray Head. Although the English reaction was disappointing, the song was a hit in America, where it sold 100,000 copies; on the strength of which, MCA invited the composers to develop it into an album. Which they duly did, in five days, in a hotel in Herefordshire. In America, the album was a bestseller, and Tim and Andrew collected their Golden Discs in January 1971. Having passed the first test, the show was now ready to face a theatre-going audience: in October, it opened on Broadway, and the following year in London, where it replaced *The Maid of the Mountains* at the Palace Theatre, and settled in for a record-breaking run. Rice and Lloyd Web-ber, who were already somewhat overwhelmed by the ease with which their master-plan had been successfully implemented, now found them-selves being acclaimed as the 'Saviours of the English Musical', which had been languishing in the wilderness ever since the fall of the prophet Bart, some ten years before.

They'd come a long way in a very short time. The partnership had been launched, by a letter, in April 1965:

11, Gunter Grove
London SW10

Dear Andrew
I have been told that you were looking for a with-it writer of lyrics for your songs, and as I have been writing pop songs for a short while now and particularly enjoy writing the lyrics, I wondered if you considered it worth your while meeting me. I may fall far short of your requirements, but anyway it would be interesting to meet up – I hope! Would you be able to get in touch with me shortly either at FLA 1822 in the evenings, or at WEL 2261 in the

Tim Rice was to fulfil a long-held ambition when he took the part of the Rock Pharaoh in a production of *Joseph and his Amazing Technicolor Dreamcoat* at the New Theatre, Oxford, in 1975

daytime (Pettit and Westlake, Solicitors, are the owners of the latter number).
Hope to hear from you.

Yours,
Tim Rice

Tim was a law student at the time, with ambitions to become a pop star. At his public school, Lancing, he'd been the lead singer in a group called 'The Aardvarks'. They weren't bad. In the school magazine, a fellow-pupil, David Hare, reported: 'The Aardvarks performed their songs with great gusto. When Rice sang "I've been cheated, I've been mistreated," he really looked as if he meant it, although I did feel that they were digging for encores, and earned them rather too easily.'

Andrew Lloyd Webber's early ambitions were of a loftier nature. Son of W. S. Lloyd Webber, Principal of the London College of Music, he started composing at the age of six. His first published work – a piano suite – appeared when he was nine. He was a Queen's Scholar at Westminster School, and then studied at the Guildhall School of Music *and* the Royal College of Music, although he recalls: 'My father was against formal training for me, and it was quite a family battle for me to get to the RCM at all. My music is largely based on what I've heard, and my father feels that an instant gift of melody can easily be educated out of people.'

Tim's letter brought them together, although for the first six months of their partnership, nothing happened. As Tim explains: 'The only reason that I'd written a song in the first place was that I wanted to be a singer. The fact that I couldn't sing very well didn't seem to be that relevant, because a lot of chaps were succeeding without being good singers. However, I thought that if I sang other writers' songs on my demo tape, it would invite unfavourable comparisons with the originals: whereas if I sang my *own* songs, then at least producers wouldn't say "He's not as good as Jagger," or whatever. But – to my amazement – the only thing that got any interest was the material, my songs. And I'd never even really thought about being a writer. Then I met Andrew, and it was he who gave me the idea of writing musicals for the theatre.'

The first fruit of their collaboration was a musical about Dr Barnardo, called *The Likes of Us*: and the very first song they wrote together (words by Rice, music by Lloyd Webber) was a chirpy love-duet, with echoes of Lionel Bart: 'Love is Here'.

The score of this early work shows the young composers to be perfectly in tune with their times, and reflecting every musical influence within earshot – from *The Sound of Music* to Tommy Steele, via Matt Monroe, *My Fair Lady*, Flanders and Swann, and Bertolt Brecht. But, inevitably, the chorus of orphan children invited comparisons with Lionel Bart's *Oliver* – which is one of the reasons why the show was never produced. Besides, Rice and Lloyd Webber were too ambitious. They turned down the offer of a production in Oxford: it was to be 'the West End or nothing' – and, in the end, nothing was what they got. *The Likes of Us* is still waiting for its first performance.

In 1967, Tim Rice gave up the law and joined EMI as a management trainee, or – as he saw it – 'a bloke who could be Sir Joseph Lockwood in thirty years' time, but meanwhile they don't know what to do with you. So you're sent round all the departments, on the road with the reps, up to the BBC to plug records.' As a result, he met Norrie Paramor, and in 1968 became his personal assistant. 'That was a lucky break, because Norrie was then one of *the* most successful record producers, and so I was able to spend a lot of time in the studios, working with Cliff Richard and the Shadows, The Scaffold and the like. These were actually hit records we were making, and I was working with success – even though the success was nil credit to me.'

He and Andrew were still getting together to write songs and, although they felt that the two-and-a-half-minute pop single was not their ideal medium, they did have the satisfaction of hearing one of their songs – 'Believe me, I Will' – on a Sacha Distel album.

In 1968 a man called Alan Doggett enters their story. He was the music master at Colet Court School in the City of London, and he commissioned Tim and Andrew to write a musical show for the school (where Andrew's younger brother was a pupil). 'At first we toyed with an idea about James Bond,' says Tim, 'but we realised that it would be something that would very quickly become dated. At the same time, I was very concerned that we should write something that the kids would enjoy the words of, because I always remember at school that the things we had to sing – like 'Men of Harlech' and all that – were great stuff, but when you're nine you don't really get much of a kick out of that kind of lyric. And then I thought of the story of Joseph and his coat of many colours, from the book of Genesis. This story was an all-time favourite of mine when I was a child, and I thought that maybe the kids of today would enjoy it too.'

He and Andrew set to work, and in three weeks produced *Joseph and the Amazing Technicolor Dreamcoat* – a twenty-minute 'pop oratorio' for choir, school orchestra, rock group and soloists. The authors, too, had

(*Overleaf*) A scene from the first West End production
of *Joseph* at the Albery Theatre, 1973

Alan Doggett, who commissioned *Joseph*

learned something from their *Likes of Us* experience: Rule One for aspiring composers of The Musical – get it *done*, no matter where. *Joseph* had its performance, at Colet Court School, in March 1968. In the audience that night was Derek Jewell, jazz and pop music critic on the *Sunday Times* – and the father of one of the boys taking part. He fell for it in a big way, and wrote in his column: 'This is a joyous, bouncing, and entirely successful piece of pop music, bursting with good tunes and clever words, yet having a musical continuity and wholeness which is quite new in the world of rock, where the differing sounds of Beatles, Cream and Doors explode and dominate. *Joseph* is, if you like, pop music moving towards its coming of age.'

The Dean of St Paul's also saw the show, and invited them to put it on in the cathedral. Norrie Paramor persuaded Decca to record it, and the album was released in the autumn. A number of 'cover versions' also appeared, of songs from the show. With a canny eye to this corner of the market, the composers had made one of the 'big numbers' sufficiently unspecific to allow it to be taken out of the context of the show, and presented as a pop single. Which it was, by Max Bygraves, Shawn Elliott, Joe Cuddy and 'Christopher'.

I closed my eyes, drew back the curtain,
To see for certain, what I thought I knew.
Far far away, someone was weeping,
But the world was sleeping:
Any dream will do. . . .

Encouraged by the success of *Joseph*, Tim and Andrew began to look for a subject for their next musical. What they lacked was the *time* in which to develop their ideas; and it was now that another fairy god-father appeared, in the form of David Land, a property tycoon with showbiz interests, manager of the Harlem Globetrotters *and* the Dagen-ham Girl Pipers. He had seen *Joseph*, liked it, and was now prepared to back his hunch that the Rice/Lloyd Webber partnership was destined for great things. For a share of their future royalties, he agreed to pay Tim and Andrew a weekly wage (initially £30) for the next three years. So Tim was able to give up his job with Norrie Paramor, and Andrew, who'd just collected his degree from the Royal College, didn't have to look for one. Instead, they became full-time songwriters.

They wrote a musical about Richard the Lionheart, 'but I think we got it slightly wrong', says Tim in retrospect. 'The important thing in a musical is to have a good, rounded story, and the plot for our *Come Back, Richard* was little more than a straight history of his reign. It didn't have a good beginning, or a strong ending – it was all a bit rambling. So after one school performance, we abandoned it.'

Then Tim heard a song by Bob Dylan which gave him an idea. Dylan sang: 'I can't think for you – you'll have to decide/Did Judas Iscariot have God on his side?' and Tim thought, why not write a musical about the relationship between Christ and Judas, and the events leading up to the crucifixion? It was a mind-boggling idea, and in the beginning both he and Andrew approached it rather tentatively. However, the Dean of St Paul's gave his blessing to the project, and the partners started to cast around for a title song. The tune came first – a simple, descending three-note phrase that dropped into Andrew's head one evening, when he was walking down the Fulham Road. He jotted it down on a napkin in Carlo's Restaurant.

The lyrics were added about two months later – just before Sunday lunch, at Tim's parents' house in Hatfield. He'd been carrying Andrew's tune around in his head, while trying to find a phrase to describe Jesus Christ, which would also fit the three-note tune. 'Originally I'd written "Jesus Christ, Jesus Christ" four times over, but I thought, "That's

David Land agreed to pay Tim and Andrew a weekly wage, and so launched them on their career as full-time songwriters

rather boring – what can I call him?" And "Superstar" scanned, so I put it in. I hadn't even heard of Warhol then – it was just a word that I'd seen once or twice in the *Melody Maker*, to describe someone like Eric Clapton, John Lennon or Mick Jagger.'

Enshrined in the lyric, and immortalised in vinyl, the epithet stuck, and *Jesus Christ, Superstar* was launched on its way to becoming one of the best-selling records of all time (the first year's gross exceeded the previous record, set by the Beatles' *Sergeant Pepper*), and a hardy perennial of the musical theatre. Sadly for the authors, this success was largely due to the American sales: the prophets, as predicted, found themselves to be 'not without honour, except in their own country'. Derek Jewell put his finger on the problem: 'Caught in the cross-fire between an older generation who may regard it as distasteful or even blasphemous, and a younger who could be deterred or scornful because of its religious associations, life is perhaps going to be hard for *Jesus Christ, Superstar.*'

Cliff Richard complained that the authors had removed all the truly religious elements from the story, thereby reducing Christ to a minor historical figure. The Dean of St Paul's saw it in a rather different light: 'There are some people who may be shocked by this record. I urge them to listen to it, and think again. It is a desperate cry – "Who are you, Jesus Christ?" is the urgent inquiry, and a very proper one at that. The record probes some answers, and makes some comparisons. The onus is on the *listener* to come up with his replies.'

In America, *Jesus Christ, Superstar* arrived at a most opportune moment. The hippie movement of the Sixties had sparked off an interest in the religions of the East. The 'mystical' writings of the Beat poets, like Ginsberg and Kerouac, and the Hindu-inspired songs of George Harrison, found a new audience, avid for 'spiritual enlightenment' in place of hallucinogenic experience. The 'Jesus freak' was preaching in the streets, and religion was *in*. Tin Pan Alley was quick to respond.

In October 1971 the *New Yorker* printed a cartoon in which a verger confronted a sad-looking vicar with a plateful of coppers, voicing the complaint: '*Jesus Christ, Superstar* has already grossed 30 million dollars. Just where did *we* go wrong?'

In Australia, the nuns of Loreto Convent found themselves in court, having staged a production of the show without permission of the copyright owners. 'Like all Christians, these nuns believe that Jesus Christ is theirs,' said the Sydney music publisher who brought the case. 'What they are forgetting is that there is such a thing as copyright.'

The final accolade came from Vatican Radio, who broadcast the album, in full. Tim Rice commented: 'When we contemplated *Jesus Christ, Superstar*, we thought that there might be resistance in Roman Catholic countries. But oddly enough it has been better received there than in Church of England areas. We think that it must be that they have a heightened awareness of religious subjects – as opposed to what can only be described as apathy in England.'

As the American royalties flooded in, Tim and Andrew were advised

The Crucifixion from *Jesus Christ,
Superstar* (Paul Nicholas as Jesus Christ)

to move out, and find a cosy tax haven where they could watch their money grow. They refused, preferring to pay tax at 83%, rather than do without the pleasures of English life, which for Andrew means the countryside, architecture and church music. For Tim, it's cricket.

In 1975, the partnership was suspended, temporarily. Andrew wanted to write a musical based on the 'Jeeves' books of P. G. Wodehouse. Initially Tim was going to write it with him – but it didn't work out. Andrew explains: 'We thought we'd do it in our usual style, which is to write everything *together* – all the music and lyrics as a complete package. Then we changed our minds, and decided it would be best to have a complete book first, before starting on the songs. At which point, Tim found it wasn't coming easily.' So he withdrew, and playwright Alan Ayckbourn stepped in. For one of the songs, Andrew recycled a tune from the ill-fated *Likes of Us*: and the cockney love-song 'Love is Here' was translated into Bertie Wooster's philosophic 'Travel Hopefully'.

For all Bertie's optimism, *Jeeves* didn't stay the course. After a disastrous try-out in Bristol, and four ill-attended weeks in London, it closed. Andrew was philosophic. The failure of *Jeeves* confirmed his view that a musical must be 'of a piece': the songs must be more than musical interludes – they should *move the story on*. His songs for *Jeeves* could have worked equally well in another context altogether – and indeed one of them did just that. The rhapsodic 'What a day – to be rolling in clover/Summer day – I'll be sad when it's over' recurs in a very different guise in *Evita*. Same tune, new lyrics: 'So what happens now? (Another suitcase in another hall)/So what happens now? (Hang your picture on another wall).'

Andrew Lloyd Webber survived his first flop with equanimity, despite the fact that his mother kept telephoning to check that he was getting enough to eat! In the comfort of his new country house (which he had bought with the proceeds from *Jesus Christ, Superstar*), he reflected on the lessons he had learnt: 'The principal one is that you must be a hundred per cent right before you go into rehearsal. *Jesus Christ, Superstar* catapulted from a recording – the basic material was there, and could not be sacrificed for commercial reasons when it came to putting on the show.'

He also announced his intention of re-forming the partnership with Tim Rice: 'We have got to get down to writing again – even if what we write never sees the light of day. We really must concentrate on what we do best; both of us are too good at finding excuses for *not* getting down to it. We had a very intense period of working together – and then it all happened, and we allowed people to come between us. It's ridiculous. Tim and I are very close, actually.'

So they got together again. Tim had just returned from Buenos Aires, with an idea for a musical about another superstar, who rose from humble origins to become frighteningly powerful – Eva Perón, known to her fans as 'Evita'. The idea was first planted in his mind by a documentary programme that he'd heard on his car radio. It was one of a series, which, the following week, was to feature James Dean.

'The fact that Eva Perón was being equated with James Dean intrigued me,' he explains, 'because although I didn't know much about *her*, I knew quite a lot about *him*. I'm interested by famous people. I don't know why. Not necessarily because I admire them. But I do find it very intriguing how they got to where they did, and why. I've no interest in boxing, but I'm fascinated by Mohammed Ali – that he should be the best-known man in the world today.

'It's interesting that some people, often for no particular reason, get elevated out of all proportion to their status – which is what I believe (without any false modesty) happened to our first work. I was fascinated, rather than thrilled, by the success of *Superstar*, and by the first tour of the US in 1971 – when the record was still a comparative failure in Britain. I couldn't believe that *Superstar* was deserving of that kind of attention – although I do still maintain immodestly that it's quite a good work.'

For Andrew, the story of *Evita* offered a solution to one of the major problems associated with musical theatre, namely 'that awkward moment when you see the conductor raising his baton, and the orchestra lurching into life during the dialogue – all of which indicates the impending approach of a song. I have a nagging feeling that the best musicals ultimately give you a sort of exhilarating experience like being in second gear in a fast car – incredibly exciting, but hardly very profound. With *Evita*, I saw the possibility of writing something where the music and words can get uninterrupted attention, without any jolts from one style to another.'

The story also provided an escape from that most familiar cliché of the musical – the Big Tune stuck in for the sake of having a Big Tune, without any particular dramatic relevance. 'The way to avoid this in *Evita* seemed fairly obvious,' explains Andrew, 'as it was possible to write music for both her public personality, and her private one. Eva Perón's public utterances range from the rabble-rousing extremist, to the slightly cynical use of sentimentality. Thus it was possible to set up a straightforwardly romantic tune in a dramatic context, in which it is valid in its own right: and immediately after her 'performance', we hear the private side of Eva, when she is only concerned with how well her

Evita in the making: Hal Prince (with glasses
on his forehead) and team following rehearsals

speech has gone down with the audience. It was this possibility of
writing about the two sides of Eva's life that made me feel that music
had a dimension to offer; and from then on I looked for "highs" and
"lows" in the story that would work dramatically and musically.'

For the next two years, the partners devoted themselves almost exclusively to their new, demanding mistress. As with *Jesus Christ, Superstar*, the plan was to make a recording of the work first, thereby ensur-
ing that the musical performance was of the highest possible standard.
The London Philharmonic Orchestra was booked, together with a cast
of star singers: Tony Christie, Colm Wilkinson, Mike d'Abo, Paul Jones,
Barbara Dickson and – in the title role – Julie Covington.

The recording took five months to complete. The finished tape was
played to an invited audience in July 1976: after which all four sides
were 're-mixed', and about fifteen minutes of material was cut or rewritten. The double album went on sale, price £5.99, in October 1976. It

had cost £90,000 to produce – 'the most expensive demo disc ever made,' as Andrew described it.

The initial response was disappointing. Although reviews were good (Derek Jewell proclaimed it to be a masterpiece), the record shops reported only moderate interest. The moguls of MCA were beginning to panic: had their Golden Boys over-reached themselves? Was it a mistake to label the new work an 'opera'? Was it too 'heavy' for the fragile structure of the Top Twenty, which in the mid-70s was being torn apart by two rival movements, echoing the Mods v. Rockers confrontation of the Sixties? This time, the polarisation was even more extreme. On one side, the 'Glitter' merchants, scorning the unadorned ordinariness of the rock 'n' roll purists, put tinsel in their hair, wore make-up and gold lamé, and used theatrical extravagance as a substitute for musical originality. On the other side of the fence, confronting the showbiz camp with obscenity, violence, and musical anarchy, stood the grisly ranks of the punk rockers.

The 'New Wave' found its audience in the new generation of teen-agers, bored and out-of-work, kicking against groups too old to identify with, concerts too expensive to attend, and songs that were no reflection of their lives. The Punk message was simple, and direct. In the curve of his guitar, Mick Jones of The Clash taped a running-order of abbreviated titles for their stage show (it never varied): London – Pressure – Bored – 1977 – Hate and War – Cheat – Remote – Police – Career – Capital – Deny – Janie Jones – Riot. Soon even the most conservative and respectable record companies were forced to associate themselves with the 'New Wave': CBS signed The Clash for £100,000, and both EMI and A&M had equally expensive honeymoons with The Sex Pistols.

Viewing these extraordinary goings-on from the sidelines, the MCA management saw little future in exposing any of the songs from 'Evita' to the hurly-burly of the Hit Parade – especially since the composers had failed to include in the score a suitably unspecific song, that might satisfactorily be lifted out of the context of the show, and presented as a pop single. However, as a trailer for the album, two songs *were* released as singles: 'Don't Cry For Me, Argentina' (sung by Julie Covington), and 'Another Suitcase in Another Hall' (sung by Barbara Dickson). 'We hoped they would get a few air-plays,' recalls Andrew, 'and so attract some publicity to the album. We never considered them to be 'hit' material: after all 'Argentina' is not the sort of song you can imagine being chanted in discos, is it?'

In the event, confounding all expectations, 'Don't Cry For Me, Argentina' sold 950,000 copies, and, eclipsing Punk and Glitter, shot to Number One. Some of the irony in the song got lost along the way, but nobody was complaining. The disc-jockeys played it incessantly: the title became a useful catch-phrase for cartoonists: and Julie Covington became a Star – although she wouldn't sing the song on TV's 'Top of the Pops'.

The success of the single gave the album a much-needed boost, and, by March 1977, it had sold 125,000 copies in Britain, and reached the Number One position in the *Melody Maker* album chart. The time had come to prepare 'Evita' for the stage. From New York, the 'King' of musical producers – Hal Prince – was summoned to take charge. A theatre, once aptly named the 'Prince Edward', was restored to its former glory after many years as a cinema. A lengthy series of auditions followed, culminating in the casting of an unknown singer – Elaine Paige – in the title role. Investors were solicited, to raise the £400,000 production budget, in £500 lots. Within days, it was over-subscribed. This remarkable display of confidence on the part of London's theatrical 'angels' was derided by the Shaftesbury Avenue pessimists, who pointed to the sorry succession of British musicals that had folded like ninepins in the preceding twelve months: *Fire Angel, Liza of Lambeth, Maggie, Kings and Clowns, Drake's Dream* – all sucked down the plug-hole of oblivion, in a matter of weeks. Who could guarantee 'Evita's' survival?

Mr Prince was asked for his views on the sorry state of the British musical. He said: 'I'm not British so maybe I'm not qualified to judge what happens here. There is fine talent around – Lionel Bart, Sandy Wilson, definitely. But somehow they don't seem to be able to keep it going. I think wherever you get a concentration of theatre, you get divisions: so-called serious theatre, and musicals, and opera, and light musicals. I think these divisions are dangerous and it doesn't happen so much in New York. I don't want to sound snobby, but some of the shows here may be a bit flimsy and superficial. I don't think anyone will say that about *Evita*.'

In the weeks before the show opened, the composers were not so confident. Remembering the negative critical response to *Jesus Christ, Superstar*, Andrew Lloyd Webber wondered whether *Evita* would get a fair hearing:

'There's no doubt about it, the English theatrical establishment gives absolutely no encouragement to the musical. Indeed, they seem to display a positive resentment towards any new writer who emerges in the musical theatre. For example, take the shit that was poured on Lionel Bart when he wrote

(Overleaf) Evita: David Essex as Che
and Elaine Paige as Evita

Evita: *Punch* cartoon by Hewison

Oliver – the press went out of their way to suggest that all the tunes were pinched. And when it turned out to be a huge commercial success, they then attacked Bart personally.

'Every so often an English musical talent comes along which is definitely capable of going on, and being developed – but this country doesn't have a tradition of musical theatre. So it's quite hard to make any progress here: and it's not always possible to uproot oneself and go off to America where they respect the musical. When a new musical opens here, you never see in the press any encouragement for the composer. It's usually "Oh Lord, another Disastrous British Musical . . ."'

This time, they got the message: and on 21 June 1978, when *Evita* was unveiled before a star-studded first-night audience, the superlatives bubbled like champagne. 'This marvellous modern opera'; 'magnificent, original, compelling'; 'Viva Evita!' Overcoming their traditional reluctance to allow that local boys might make good, the critics were unanimous in saluting *Evita* as the crowning achievement of the

186

Rice/Lloyd Webber partnership. The musical score, according to Derek Jewell, 'proves Lloyd Webber to be the most remarkable musical child of his generation. He has heard much, sensitively absorbed it, and produced his own completely original and personal synthesis.' The lyrics show Tim Rice to be the undisputed master of the throwaway line, and the apt juxtaposition: 'from the bars, from the back streets, from the gutter theatrical' – 'the biggest social climber since Cinderella' – 'she's a diamond in their dull grey lives/and that's the hardest kind of stone, it usually survives'. Together, they've re-awakened in the minds of jaded pop-marketeers (motto: 'Art for Art's sake, and Money for God's sake') the notion that work of quality, without hype or compromise, might actually have some appeal to the listening public.

'Is *Evita* the end?' asked the *Daily Express*, in July 1978, noting that 'rumours of friction, rows and walk-outs suggest that this might be the last production that Rice and Lloyd Webber will ever do together'. But

Tim Rice and Andrew Lloyd Webber watch rehearsals with David Land

187

manager David Land remained philosophical: 'They are two highly volatile, creative people. They're vastly different personalities, and there are bound to be frictions and rows. Occasionally, they even hate each other. Tim is relaxed and cricket-loving. Andrew is intense and absorbed in his work. Feelings are bound to run high all the time. One day, Tim arrived late for some *Evita* rehearsals. Andrew asked him where the hell he'd been, and Tim replied: "At the Test Match." The row ended with them both storming out, and me being left with a stunned orchestra! But I think they'll work together again – given that a really good idea comes up.'

Meanwhile, they've gone their separate ways. There are rumours of a musical about the 'Bay of Pigs' fiasco – but more cynical observers of the shifting trends that dictate the course of popular music can see the writing on the wall. The Seventies are drawing to a close, the 'Superstar' is burning out. The 1980s loom, and the outlook is grim. Orwell's 1984 . . . the Ministry of Truth . . . computerised pop music broadcast by the Music Department . . . songs composed without human intervention: bland, featureless, instantly forgettable. . . .

Eddie's Club in Liverpool, February 1979, provides a glimpse into the future as appalling as Orwell's fiction. An audience of teenage unemployed works itself into a parody of frenzied excitement, while on stage a tubby singer, with braces on her teeth, sporting a bandsman's uniform (shades of Sergeant Pepper?), sings: 'I wanna be Insta-matic, I wanna be a frozen pea.' The singer calls herself Poly Styrene, and she writes all her own songs. She sings mostly on one note, and her theme is equally singular. Impermanence, ephemerality – and music to suit the times. Disposable music. Throwaway music. Junk.

Acknowledgements

PICTURE CREDITS

Picture Research by Naomi Narod

Page 6 Radio Times Hulton Picture Library; 10 Christine Mayhew, photo Derrick Witty; 12 Mander & Mitchenson Theatre Collection; 15 Manchester Public Library; 18 Radio Times Hulton Picture Library; 20 The Walker Art Gallery, Liverpool; 22 Radio Times Hulton Picture Library; 23 Radio Times Hulton Picture Library; 25 Mander & Mitchenson Theatre Collection; 27 Radio Times Hulton Picture Library; 29 Theatre Museum of the Victoria and Albert Museum, photo Derrick Witty; 30 Radio Times Hulton Picture Library; 32 Dorothy Miskin; 34 Mander & Mitchenson Theatre Collection; 35 Mander & Mitchenson Theatre Collection; 36 Radio Times Hulton Picture Library; 38 Radio Times Hulton Picture Library; 39 Radio Times Hulton Picture Library; 41 Dudley Scholte; 44 Radio Times Hulton Picture Library; 46–7 Theatre Museum of the Victoria and Albert Museum, photo Derrick Witty; 49 Radio Times Hulton Picture Library; 50 Mander & Mitchenson Theatre Collection; 52 Radio Times Hulton Picture Library; 53 Radio Times Hulton Picture Library; 56 Mander & Mitchenson Theatre Collection; 59 Photo Files; 61 Mander & Mitchenson Theatre Collection; 62 Mander & Mitchenson Theatre Collection; 63 Bodleian Library, Oxford, courtesy *The Tatler*; 64 Mander & Mitchenson Theatre Collection; 66 Radio Times Hulton Picture Library; 67 Bodleian Library, Oxford, courtesy *The Tatler*; 69 Radio Times Hulton Picture Library; 71 Mander & Mitchenson Theatre Collection; 72 Mander & Mitchenson Theatre Collection; 75 Radio Times Hulton Picture Library; 76 Radio Times Hulton Picture Library; 78–9 *Melody Maker*; 81 Radio Times Hulton Picture Library; 85 *Melody Maker*; 87 Culver Pictures; 88 Photo Files; 91 Photo Files; 92 Keystone Press Agency; 94 Mander & Mitchenson Theatre Collection; 97 Theatre Museum of the Victoria and Albert Museum, photo Derrick Witty; 98–9 Kobal Collection; 101 Courtesy National Film Archive Stills Library, the Rank Organisation Ltd; 103 Mander & Mitchenson Theatre Collection; 104 Bodleian Library, Oxford, courtesy *The Tatler*; 106 Mander & Mitchenson Theatre Collection; 107 Theatre Museum of the Victoria and Albert Museum, photo Derrick Witty; 109 Theatre Museum of the Victoria and Albert Museum, photo Derrick Witty; 110 Mander & Mitchenson Theatre Collection; 113 BBC; 115 Theatre Museum of the Victoria and Albert Museum, photo Derrick Witty; 118 Anthony Buckley; 120 Keystone Press Agency; 122 BBC Pictorial Publicity; 125 Report, photo Alan Vines; 127 Courtesy Manager Garrick Theatre (*Daily Express* photo, William Lovelace); 129 Reproduced by permission of *Punch*; 131 Reg Wilson; 132 Reproduced by permission of *Punch*; 133 Zoë Dominic; 135 Reproduced by permission of *Punch*; 136–7 Rex Features; 140 Leslie Bryce; 143 The Press Association; 144 Keystone Press Agency; 148 Reproduced by permission from *The Beatles*; The authorised biography by Hunter Davies © Hunter Davies 1968; 150 Rex Features; 151 Keystone Press Agency; 152 Robert Freeman; 154–5 Keystone Press Agency; 159 EMI Records (UK); 160–1 Keystone Press Agency;

SONG CREDITS